Looking Up

Looking Up

by

Jim N. Griffith

Mercer University Press
Macon, Georgia

ISBN 0-86554-427-1

Looking Up
Copyright ©1993
Mercer University Press, Macon, Georgia 31207
Printed in the United States of America

The paper used in this publication meets the minimum requirements
of American National Standard for Information Sciences—
Permanence of Paper for Printed Library Materials, ANSI Z39.48–1984.

Library of Congress Cataloging-in-Publication Data

Griffith, Jim N.
    Looking up / by Jim N. Griffith.
    xii+185pp. 6x9" (15x22cm.).
    ISBN 0-86554-427-1 (alk. paper).
    1. Christian life—Baptist authors. I. Title.
BV4501.2.G75825   1993
248.4'861—dc20   93-14384
                                                              CIP

Contents

Preface

Sadly, this is an age in which so many persons live down in the doldrums rather than on the mountaintops of life. Confronted with what they feel are insurmountable problems, they spend their lives looking down rather than looking up. It is regrettable that many live at the low point rather than the high point of life.

Like the man who spent his life looking down at the ground and found only a few coins, paper clips, and scraps of paper, we often pass up the true treasures of life because we do not raise our horizons and "lift our eyes to the hills of faith and strength from whence cometh our help." It is my hope and desire that these pages provide a walk through life that will look up in faith rather than down in futility.

This book is written for the express purpose of enabling every reader in every walk of life to have the joy of looking up.

—*Jim N. Griffith*

Dedication

This book is affectionately dedicated to all fellow seekers of the happy life; to those who have looked at life through the eyes of faith—looking above the dangers, toils, snares, and tears—to the teachings of the One who said, "I have come that your joy might be full." (John 15:11) This is "looking up" in the finest sense of the word.

Acknowledgments

Appreciation is expressed to Mercer University Press and to the *Christian Index*, which first published many of these writings.

Special gratitude is also expressed to Cathy Humphrey, who graciously took on the task of compiling and indexing the book which serves to enhance its usefulness for the reader who is searching for a particular subject.

—*J.N.G.*

A New and Happy Day

The place: a large Western city. The time: a gloomy Monday morning.

The elevator in a busy office building was overflowing with people—most of whom were wearing glum expressions on their faces.

Suddenly, as the elevator car started up, the operator began humming a lively tune and dancing a little jig.

One passenger seemed particularly irritated by the man's pleasant mood and snapped, "What have you got to be so happy about today?"

"Well, sir," replied the man happily, "I ain't never lived this day before."

Fortunately, there are a good many persons who have found the victory in life, claiming for themselves the biblical note: "This is the day which the Lord has made. We will rejoice and be glad in it." (Psalm 118:24)

They are determined to be so strong that nothing can disturb their peace of mind, knowing full well that their strength is in the Lord.

They look at the sunny side of everything—undergirded by the sure knowledge that Jesus said: "These things I have spoken unto you, that in me ye might have peace. In the world ye shall have tribulation: but be of good cheer; I have overcome the world." (John 16:33)

These gifted persons are somehow able to think only of the best, to work for the best and expect only the best.

They join the apostle Paul in declaring: "Finally, brethren, whatsoever things are true, whatsoever things are honest, whatsoever things are just, whatsoever things are pure, whatsoever things are lovely, whatsoever things are of good report; if there be any virtue, and if there be any praise, think on these things." (Philippians 4:8)

Because of their victorious attitude toward life, they add to the day's supply of joy.

In season and out of season, they practice the fine art of looking up.

Don't Forget to Laugh

Laughter has been called "the best medicine."

I do know that in the Bible, Proverbs 17:22 reminds us that "a merry heart doeth good like a medicine."

Sad, though it may be, all indications support the conclusion that in this harried and hurried day, many persons have lost their sense of humor.

In many cases, a scowl has replaced a smile and a groan has taken the place of a grin.

Even though medical studies have shown that there is healing power in laughter, some still refuse to take advantage of this boon to good health.

According to Dr. Hendrie Weisenger, "If your daily total of laughs is less than fifteen—including three belly laughs—you are underlaughed."

Laughter not only aids digestion, I am told, but it also is a "pain-reliever."

For example, if you will laugh more, it may keep you from being a pain in the neck to others.

Weisenger further states: "Laughter is a form of physical and mental fitness that provides lots of accumulated exercise throughout the day."

Presumably, you could think of it as a form of "internal jogging."

Being able to see the humor in a difficult time is a tension-reliever and often proves to be a blessing to many.

There is always enough trouble and sadness to go around.

But there can never be enough laughter and good cheer unless we are willing to share what we have.

As someone has wisely said, "If you didn't start out the day with a smile, it's not too late to start practicing for tomorrow."

God's Kind of Love

What is mankind's greatest fear?

Some would suggest that it is war or serious illness. Others would say mankind's greatest fear is to be hungry, destitute, or in unbearable pain. But as terrible as these fears are, they may not be man's worst fear.

Bennett Cerf, who served for many years as one of the panelists on the popular television program "What's My Line?" was once asked, "What are you most afraid of?" He replied, "I have to admit that the thing I am most afraid of is not being loved."

Deep within the hearts of many persons, the same fear persists. To love and to be loved is still the greatest deed and joy of mankind.

In Margaret Walker's novel *Jubilee*, Vyvy the mother, speaks of her commitment to love: "Keeping hatred inside makes you get mean and evil inside. We are supposed to love everybody like God loves us.

"And when you forgive, you feel sorry for the one who hurt you, you return love for hate, and good for evil. And that stretches your heart and makes you bigger inside with a bigger heart so that you can love everybody. You can lick the world with a loving heart."

Underline the mother's words: *We are supposed to love everybody like God loves us.*

Did you hear about the classified ad that read something like this: "Lost Dog. Reward offered. Brown hair, turning gray around the mouth. Right leg broken when struck by an automobile. Arthritis in left hip. Blind in right eye. Tail broken in two joints. Answers to the name of Lucky."

Lucky? In view of all that has taken place in the life of this dog, some might question the appropriateness of his name.

But, of course, he *was* a lucky dog! He was lucky because, with all those things wrong with him, somebody still wanted him, still loved him, and was willing to pay to get him back.

Isn't that the essence of the good news of the gospel? With all of our sins, rebellion, and imperfections, God still loves us enough to pay the ultimate price to win us back to Himself.

And that's God's kind of love.

Don't Concentrate on Falling

The late great aerialist Carl Wallenda put his own trademark on his performance as a tightrope walker by working 125 feet in the air without a net.

There was no question about his dedication to his chosen field. "For me," he declared, "walking the tightrope is everything."

He summarized his feelings by saying: "Everything else is just waiting."

It is sad to report that some years ago during a performance in San Juan, Puerto Rico, the Great Wallenda fell to his death.

When questioned about the reason for this unfortunate mishap, Wallenda's widow said that through the years he had always had absolute concentration, but on this one particular day he became preoccupied with falling rather than walking the wire to the other side.

There is a lesson in this for all of us: Keep your eye on the goal rather than the fall.

The apostle Paul said: "This one thing I do. . . . " (Philippians 3:12)

Total commitment and concentration will help each of us to avoid the dangers of indecision and destruction.

There is still another pertinent fact worthy of note by each of us. For "tightrope walking" over any of the dangerous chasms of life, balance is a necessity.

This much is certain: Even in this unusual day noted for sleight of hand and quick of foot, no one has ever been able to cross the chaotic chasms of life on the first bounce.

However, it is heartening to remember that Christians in perilous places do have a net. The Scripture affirms it: "The eternal God is thy refuge, and underneath are the everlasting arms." (Deuteronomy 33:27)

But even above that is another word from Scripture (Ephesians 6:13) that speaks to all of the hazardous crossings of life: "and having done all, to stand."

Loving and Living over the Long Haul

Fred Craddock, in an address to ministers, touched on the practical applications of consecration.

"To give my life for Christ is glorious," he said.

"To pour myself out for others—to pay the ultimate price—I'll do it, Lord," Craddock declared, "I'm ready to go out in a blaze of glory."

This well-known professor of preaching and popular lecturer reminded us that too often we think giving our all to the Lord is like taking a $1,000 bill and laying it on the table with the words: "Here's my life, Lord, I'm giving it all."

But this, according to Craddock, is not the reality of the situation.

Actually, life is more like the Lord sending us to the bank to cash in the $1,000 bill for quarters and fifty-cent pieces, and having us go through life putting our twenty-five cents here and fifty cents there as we apply little deeds of Christian kindness to all the needs of life.

He says: "It's patiently listening to the troubles of your fellow man instead of saying 'Get lost!'"

There are other ways we spend our lives: going to countless committee meetings, loving the unlovely, offering a word of Christian encouragement, being faithful in our Christian witness, or giving a cup of cold water to a lonely old person in a nursing home.

Giving our life for Christ isn't always like going out in a blaze of glory. In fact, many times it is more like "hanging in there," keeping on keeping on, persevering to the end.

It happens in all those little acts of unselfish Christian love.

The joy comes when we cash in all the glory for the greater but smaller change of living the Christian life little by little over the long haul.

Present—Tense; Future—Perfect

The road-to-Emmaus experience, following the crucifixion and resurrection of Christ, speaks to us after we have passed through the observance of Easter.

We, too, are moving along troubled roads of life—and often we are unaware that the living Christ walks with us.

Many are moving along roads, trying to face facts, living with bleak reality—and a phrase that comes from school lessons in grammar is applicable now for the prevailing mood and immediate prospect: "present-tense."

But what of the future? There is no doubt about the tensions of the present: discouragement, even despair. This was also true of the travelers trudging along the road to Emmaus as they moaned: "What kind of world is this? Jesus crucified on a cross—and we were so sure that if anyone could have saved us, it was this Jesus."

And then it happened: the discouraged travelers were joined along the road by the risen Jesus, who is the answer to their every need.

If this scriptural event means to the despondent Emmaus travelers that death and evil could not defeat or hold Christ, then it means the same for us if we are linked to Christ by faith.

It means, in so many words, that for all who trust Christ, love him and serve him—it can be a case of present-tense, but future-perfect.

Certainly tensions are with us. In this kind of world Christians cannot escape tension.

But if you commit yourself to God in Christ, commit all that you know of yourself to all that you know of the Lord, you can experience release from many inner tensions.

More than ever, the Christian must be the light and salt that can set us free from despair.

This is the fact, the claim, the promise, and the truth of the resurrection: "Present-tense"—situation hopeless from man's perspective; but from Christ's standpoint, the situation is never hopeless, and that is "Future-perfect."

Don't Judge the Day by the Weather

Many have expressed joy and satisfaction that spring is finally here.

But every month in the year can be a lovely month, if we look at each day through the eyes of a child.

A little girl finished her breakfast prayer with these words, "And we thank you, God, for this beautiful day." After she said "Amen," her mother chided her for her seeming insincerity.

"It's not a beautiful day," said the mother. She reminded the child how cold, dark, rainy, and blustery it was outside.

"But Mother," replied the daughter, "it is a beautiful day." And then, with childlike wisdom, she said, "Mother, don't ever judge a day by the weather!"

When we look at God's beautiful creations through grateful eyes, we can realize that every month is beautiful, regardless of weather. We can see that every person is special regardless of imperfections and that every circumstance is filled with possibilities for good, regardless of difficulties.

So, remember this: Do not judge any day by the weather. Don't be guilty of just looking on the surface of things. Look at life through the beautiful windows of joy and gratitude to God for his many blessings to us.

In spite of changes all about us, there is constancy in God's love and strength.

The old hymn expresses it well in declaring that no matter what the weather or the climate of our times may be, we can stand strong in the faith.

Swift to its close ebbs out life's little day;
Earth's joys grow dim, its glories pass away;
Change and decay in all around I see:
O Thou who changest not, abide with me!

Any Way You Say It:
Here Is Good and Glad News

As has often been the case, a new Sunday school teacher in the children's department had to straighten out class members' problems with the Lord's Prayer.

One child had to be corrected after repeating, "Howard be Thy name."

Another youngster prayed, "Lead us not into Penn Station."

Still another class member surprised the teacher with "Our Father, Who art in heaven. How did you know my name? . . . "

It's obvious from this that glimmers of great truths often come from childish interpretations.

God does know our name. He knows each of us and loves each of us as if there were only one of us.

We agree with the child in the wonder of it all. Nonetheless, our Father in heaven knows our name, knows us as we are, and yet loves us.

When I reflect on other interpretations and observations of children, I always come back to one of my favorites: the little girl who quoted the twenty-third Psalm in her own original marvelous way.

Said she: "The Lord is my Shepherd—that's all I need."

One could say it more accurately, but one could not say it more effectively.

In the midst of all the crying needs of a confused and lost world, there is but one universal need and one answer to that need.

The child has reminded us that the answer to the needs of every life is not in self, but in the Savior. For there is salvation in no other.

Let ears be unstopped and hear. Let eyes be opened to see and hearts receive the good and glad news: "The Lord is my Shepherd—that's all I need."

Giving Yourself

We are all familiar with large containers found in shopping centers and used by Salvation Army, Goodwill Industries, and other such organizations for the purpose of collecting donations of used clothing.

Not long ago, according to a television network newscaster, a passerby heard a fellow crying for help from inside one of those receptacles.

Astonishing as it may seem, someone was trapped inside.

Believe it or not, the unfortunate fellow said he fell in while opening the chute to deposit a bundle of clothes.

Admittedly, it is difficult to comprehend. But I can see how it could happen—especially to a small fellow who may have gotten carried away with his enthusiasm for stuffing a bundle of clothing inside.

Be that as it may, you would have to say that, even though it was by accident, he did give himself along with clothes.

There is much truth in the saying that "the gift without the giver is bare."

And it is equally true that giving yourself is the most precious gift you can give.

I recall the incident of the busy young woman from a church who rushed by a nursing home one afternoon to leave some literature from the church office for one of the elderly church members who lived in the home.

She was in such a hurry that she hardly paused as she placed the literature on the table, turned toward the door, and hesitated only long enough to say: "Anything else I can do for you?"

The little old lady tried to manage a smile as she looked up from her wheelchair and said: "Yes, the next time you come to see me—try leaving a little more of yourself."

It is true: The gift without the giver is bare.

As the Scripture says: "They first gave themselves."

Seeing the Possibilities

Stephanie, our granddaughter, was spending the weekend with us. Bedtime came, and I went with her upstairs to hear her prayers.

I knelt beside her, and she began to pray. It was an unselfish prayer. She remembered all of her loved ones. Then she prayed: "Lord, help us to realize that there is some good in everyone."

Grandfatherly pride notwithstanding, I had to rate this little girl's prayer pretty high on the scale of great prayers I have heard.

In fact, long after she had gone to sleep, I found myself repeating the prayer, "Lord, help me to see that there is some good in everyone."

I do know this: The world has been made a better place by those who seek to discover the hidden possibilities in others.

Luther Burbank, the horticulturist, was once asked what he considered his greatest contribution to be, and he answered: "If I have made any worthy contribution, it is the advancement and proof of the great principle in botany that a plant, born of a weed, or a plant degenerated by the conditions of nature, does not have to remain a degenerate. I have enunciated the principle that there is no plant so great an outcast that it cannot with skill and care be redeemed."

The principle holds true in botany; it holds true in people. No person has to remain the way he or she is. Change is possible through the redemptive power of Christ.

The gospels remind us that Jesus saw greatness in persons He met and brought it out.

That was true of Zacchaeus, the greedy tax gatherer everyone hated. When Jesus looked up into the sycamore tree, He saw possibilities in Zacchaeus and brought out the best in him.

This is redemption. This is evangelism which begins with seeing the possibilities in our fellowman.

So, may each of us join in making this our prayer: "Lord, help us to realize that there is some good in everyone."

Excuses

When a child misses school for one or more days, parents are required in most school districts to send a written excuse as an explanation for the student's absence from class.

The excuses are often amusing. Here, for example, are samples of actual excuses:

"Johnny was absent yesterday because of a sore *trout*."

(One could not blame the teacher for suspecting that there was something fishy about this excuse.)

"Please excuse Freddie for being out yesterday because he had the *fuel*."

Two other excuses are on the drastic side, to say the least.

"Please excuse Janie for being absent. She was sick and I had her shot."

"My son is under a doctor's care and should not take *fiscal* education. Please excuse him."

We smile at these excuses for children, but we must admit that adults are past masters at excusing themselves.

I read somewhere that the annual convention of the Hypochondriac Society was held last month, but all of the members phoned in excuses and said they were too sick to attend.

It was the same story with the Procrastinators Convention. They wanted to meet, but couldn't get around to it.

Excuses also afflict us in the spiritual realm. "And they all with one consent began to make excuse." (Luke 14:18)

If one really wants to make an excuse for not being all that he should be to God and man, it can be woven from the flimsiest thread.

But the fact remains, as the writer warns us:

Of all sad words of tongue and pen,
The saddest are these: it might have been.

A wiser course to follow is that we swap our faltering excuses for greater commitment.

Terrible Twos

Parents with small children who seem "to get into everything" have often referred to this troublesome time as the "terrible twos." Toddlers, now walking and tall enough to reach all kinds of interesting objects and yet too young to understand what is forbidden, give parents a hard time. A pastor, however, insists that there are additional "terrible twos"—not necessarily limited to small children.

It all comes in twos. Although the Sunday bulletin announces only one service at 11 a.m., in reality there are two services, both at 11 o'clock.

According to some, one service is too formal, has too many old and slow hymns, and seems to drag. The other service, some say, is too informal, has too much loud modern music, and is not worshipful.

The preacher also preaches two sermons at this single 11 o'clock service: the one he thinks meets the need of the congregation—well prepared and concise. It is the same sermon some members describe as "dull, lifeless, and far too long."

Almost every church also has two congregations—each different in nature. Some visitors say: "Oh, what a wonderful, warm and friendly congregation you have. Everyone made me feel so welcome."

Others say: "This is the coldest church I have ever had the misfortune to attend—I was here last Sunday and nobody even spoke to me."

Such are the terrible twos. Pastors can also give supporting evidence that the church has two bulletins—although only one is handed out on Sunday morning.

There is the one that people read which contains all necessary announcements and information and the one nobody reads—especially those who complain, "I didn't know we were having that—I didn't see it in the bulletin."

Most churches also have two sets of members—ones who are always there—and others who are never there.

In the "terrible twos," it all comes down to two attitudes of commitment: one says, "Jesus and the church don't mean much to me," and the other joyfully exclaims, "The Lord and my church mean everything to me."

Communication, Togetherness, and Unity

Operating in the midst of some of the tensions of our day has a tendency to make some feel like the Christian in the arena with the lion.

The Christian is convinced that if he can just communicate with the lion, his life will be spared.

He starts talking, and in a moment he hears the lion mumbling.

"Thank God!" the Christian exclaims, "we're communicating."

To which the lion replies, "I don't know about you, but I'm saying grace."

Communication is not always as valuable as it appears to be—nor is togetherness.

G. Roland Rabon in *Proclaim* magazine says: "One night when I was a boy, my dad took me coon hunting, and during the hunt, we caught a possum.

"I talked Dad into allowing me to take the unhappy animal home, where I put it in a fifty-gallon barrel and covered the top with screen wire.

"Later, wishing for some excitement, I dropped my sister's cat into the barrel to find out how a cat and possum would get along occupying the same limited space.

"The barrel began to shake as growls and shrieks echoed from the barrel.

"In an instant, the cat sprang out of the barrel, and on the second bounce landed on top of the pumphouse, where he sat, licking his body and nursing his skinned head."

The truth learned that day was that there was plenty of communication and togetherness in the barrel, but there was certainly no unity or fellowship.

When God's people gather in the Lord's church to do the Lord's business, there must be more than communication and togetherness. There must be, in obedience to Christ, a unity of spirit as well as a unity of purpose.

If we could regain and recapture the true spirit of Christian love and the unity that existed in the early church where "they were all together in one place," a new day could dawn in all churches.

Rules for Living

All of us would do well to find and follow good rules for living.

One of the most famous educators was Alice Freeman Palmer, who was known as "the Ambassador of Sunshine."

When conducting a roundtable discussion one day, she was asked to reveal the secret of her cheerfulness.

"I will give you three simple rules," she replied.

"First, you commit something to memory every day—something good." This could be a verse of Scripture, a biblical thought that puts iron into spiritually tired blood.

"Second, look for something fine every day."

I like this. Look on the bright side. Admittedly, there is much that's bad clouding the horizon. But there is also much good about life for which we can rejoice and be grateful.

Look for the positive. Look for the good in life and look for the good in others and "make certain that you do this every single day or it will not work," according to this rule for living.

"Third, do something for somebody else every day—every day!"

These are three simple but excellent rules for living.

It is true that those who seem to have found the greatest joy in life are those who find their joy in helping others.

Doing for others is the investment in kindness and consideration that always bears rich dividends.

The dividends that return are not monetary, but returns are those that satisfy the soul.

These are the dividends that can be counted when one is old, takes inventory of a well-spent life, and is comforted to find that in following the Christian way one did the unselfish thing, discovering that the Scripture is correct: "It is more blessed to give than to receive."

The Missing Ingredient in Preaching

When I think of Abraham Lincoln and church and preachers, I always recall his classic comment:

"When a preacher is preaching to me," he said, "I want him to look like he's fighting bees."

But some time ago, I came across another Lincoln comment which is even more essential to what we would call good and effective preaching.

It is said that President Lincoln frequently attended the New York Avenue Presbyterian Church on Wednesday evenings.

It was a simpler time when he could slip out through the side door of the White House and in through the side door of the church without a company of secret service men.

Lincoln purposely chose Wednesday evenings so as not to disturb the Sunday worship service, and the pastor left the study door unlocked when he knew the president was coming so Mr. Lincoln could sit in the study off to the right of the auditorium, leave the door open, and listen to Dr. Phineas Gurley.

On one particular Wednesday evening, while walking back to the White House, his aide asked President Lincoln to give his appraisal of the sermon.

The president, pausing a moment to give thought to his reply, said: "The content was excellent, and he delivered it with eloquence. It's apparent that he had put much time and effort into preparing the message."

"Then you thought it was a great sermon?" questioned the aide.

"No," replied Lincoln.

"But," protested the aide, "you said—"

"I know," Lincoln said, "but Dr. Gurley forgot the most important ingredient. He forgot to ask us to do something great."

He who aims at nothing usually hits it.

Perhaps we should add to helpful homiletical hints this significant word for the preacher:

Always ask your congregation to do something great for God.

Songs in the Night

Someone once asked the searching question: "How much would you do for others if you knew there was no possibility of reward, no anticipated expression of appreciation, and little chance of anyone ever hearing of the good deed you had done?"

This is a good question, and it brings us face to face with an examination of what motivates us to serve others.

To help without any thought of recognition or reward except that we know we do our Lord's will still brings deep and durable satisfaction.

William Barclay told the story of the famous minister and poet, George Herbert.

On his way to a gathering of a little group of musician friends who often played together in what today's youngsters would call a "combo," he passed a driver whose wagon was stuck.

With no thought of his engagement nor his immaculate clothes, Mr. Herbert immediately slid down into the muddy ditch and went to work in an effort to help the unfortunate driver pull out the cart.

Both working together, they finally succeeded, but only after Mr. Herbert was literally covered with mud and very late for his meeting.

When at last he did arrive for his engagement with his friends, he explained his appearance and why he was so late.

"You are too late, now," said one of his fellow musicians, "You have missed the music."

"Yes," said Herbert, quietly reflecting on his act of kindness, "But I shall have songs at midnight."

When we look back across our days, will there be some deep joy in the thought that we have tried to help our fellowman?

There are some who go through life "passing by on the other side" and ignoring needs of others. But when we, in the spirit of Christ, serve others, we do have our songs in the night and in the day, too.

Measuring Maturity

A mother of a four-year-old received a note from his teacher that read as follows:

"I think you should know that Johnny has a problem—he is so immature."

"Immature?" exclaimed the mother. "If you can't be immature at four years of age, when can you be?"

This is a good question. But the problem with most of us is that immaturity is not limited to four-year-olds.

Maturity, although desperately needed, is not always easily found in this day.

Ralph Waldo Emerson defined maturity "as the ability to control anger and settle differences without violence or destruction.

"Maturity is perseverance and the ability to sweat out a project or a situation in spite of opposition and discouraging setbacks.

"Maturity is unselfishness—responding first to the needs of others.

"Maturity is the capacity to face unpleasantness, discomfort, and defeat, without complaint or collapse.

"Maturity is the ability to make a decision and stand by it.

"Maturity means dependability: keeping one's word, and coming through in a crisis."

It might also be said that maturity begins with commitment—commitment to the will and way of Christ.

An anonymous poet expressed it in this way:

If God can make a tiny seed
Into a flower so fair,
What can He make, O Soul, of thee,
Through study, faith, and prayer?

Steady or Motionless?

A speaker at the Texas Evangelism Conference rebuked "Christian leaders who are living for the first and the fifteenth."

"I'm up to my ears," he said, "with those who don't want to work."

If not the proverbial nail, the statement does hit the truth on the nose. There is no substitute for hard work.

The God who called us, the church or denominational agency we serve—all have a right to expect from us our best work.

With passing years, personality may dim, cleverness can fade, showmanship can sour, but honest, hard work prevails.

A young man, who was always ready to quit at the slightest suggestion of hard work, moved from one job to another.

Seeking help at an employment agency, he left an application on file with a kindly woman who promised to do all she could.

Phoning a former employer, she asked for some information about his work habits.

"Tell me," she asked, "Was this young man a steady worker?"

"Steady?" he replied, "Why, he was not only steady—he was motionless!"

There may be others who fall into the "motionless" category. But Jesus reminded us in Scripture that we are to work.

"Work," our Lord said, "for the night is coming when no man can work." It is obvious from the life and ministry of Jesus that He expected his followers to work.

For those who would deny themselves, take up their crosses, and follow Christ, work is not an option, but an imperative.

It may be true as it was said of one minister: "He was incomprehensible on Sunday and invisible Monday through Saturday."

However, it is no less true that many laypersons want to exercise little more than their authority. They are happy to do anything for the Lord—so long as it is in an advisory capacity.

But for the called of God, the choice was made when the call was extended and accepted.

Jesus charted the course for all of us when He said: "I must—I must work the works of him that sent me."

Remembering to Say Thank You

Have you ever considered the large assembly of the great unthanked people who have touched your life in some helpful way?

It is something we all need to do, for it often leads to a meaningful exercise in the fine art of expressing gratitude.

A few years ago someone mentioned my first-grade teacher, and it called to mind warm and pleasant memories. I remembered this sweet and pretty lady who loved that class of frightened little youngsters.

As I wrote her to say "thank you," I could still remember the reassurance of her undeserved hug bestowed upon a little boy caught up in a big, new, unfamiliar world called school.

I remembered and wrote to the first Sunday school director in the church of my early boyhood.

I thanked him for his faithfulness and his commitment, which were an example to others. Fortunately, my expression of gratitude reached him a short while before he went to heaven.

There was the high school teacher who first encouraged me to try a bit of writing. A long time ago, I made known my appreciation.

I reflected on a wonderful college professor. He was a man without guile who blessed my life. I thanked him for it.

Then, there was one of my pastors in particular. With appreciation, I remembered his loving spirit, his gift of encouragement, his hearty laugh. I'm glad I told him so.

Also, there were seminary professors who influenced my life. I sent letters of gratitude.

And then, this past Christmas I heard of the serious illness of the first chairman of deacons in my first pastorate. I hastened to write him to say how much he had meant to me in my early ministry.

If I ever achieved any success, I told him he would deserve much of the credit.

It is a good thing to find a way to thank the great host of unthanked people of your past.

Did not the apostle Paul say, "in everything give thanks?"

Make the Best of It

All who surrender to the daily practice of pessimism would have us join them in thinking that the world is rapidly traveling on a path that leads to ruin. But with the knowledge that God is in his heaven, we do not have to follow the pessimist's plan of majoring on misery.

There may be a few persons who "enjoy poor health" or at least the satisfaction of complaining about it—just as there are those who specialize in circulating bad news.

But do not let the dismal news of the day deceive you. There are many fine people in this world, and they do thousands of good things every day.

Furthermore, there are millions of persons who seem to have perfected the fine art of making the best of life—no matter what happens.

More of us might do well to copy the spunk and spark of the young farm boy in a cornfield who was approached one day by a man driving through the country.

He stopped and said, "It looks like all your corn is turning yellow."

"Yes," said the boy, "we planted yellow corn."

"Well," said the man, "it looks to me like you're not going to get but about half a crop."

"That's right," said the boy, "we planted on halves."

In anger the man shouted, "You are not far from a fool, are you, son?"

"No, sir," he said, "just a fence between us."

It is foolish to always look on the darker side of life. I prefer to stand with the great old Christian lady of faith who, despite what seemed to be insurmountable problems, offered this daily prayer: "Lord, if you'll furnish the grace, I'll furnish the grit."

Don't Climb the Wall

As one goes from church to church, it is interesting to note the various inscriptions on church signs.

Some are amusing. One, I recall, in front of the church auditorium listed—I suppose—the preacher's sermon topic: "You Don't Know What Hell Is."

And then, right underneath were the words: "Come and hear our choir."

We must not assume, of course, any connection between the two inscriptions.

Sometimes a church sign triggers other thoughts. For example, there was a neatly painted sign, designed to protect the flowers and vine growing near a brick wall at one end of a church parking lot that read: "Don't Climb the Wall."

This is good advice in any event.

When life gets too complicated, when circumstances seem to be closing in upon us, when problems get too pressing, there are some who feel like "climbing the wall."

But Christian faith shows us how we can triumph over difficulties, overcome adversities, and adjust to less-than-perfect conditions.

There is no need to "climb the wall" if only we will be still, come into God's presence and trust in His goodness, love, and guidance.

With Christ leading the way, we can calmly walk through the door of opportunity with confidence, faith, and assurance, and enter into the joy and serenity of abundant life.

Don't climb the wall.

Instead, do this: Stand firm with both feet planted on the solid ground of faith.

With God You Can

An old saying has it that *"Can't* never did anything." But this is not exactly right. *Can't* has done plenty.

Down through the centuries, *can't* has stifled enthusiasm, sabotaged dreams, and impeded progress. *Can't*, the Goliath of discouragement, has wounded countless victims and left them stranded on the battlefield of life. But there are three smooth stones of affirmation which, if they find their mark like David's missile, can prove to be the conqueror of Giant Can't. The words are: Sure You Can.

However, these words are made more effective when preceded by two more powerful all-conquering words: with God; for, "with God," it is always Sure You Can.

In the strength of Almighty God, let these affirmations be yours:

With God, no mountain is too high to climb—not when one looks to the Mount Everest of faith.

With God, no obstacle is too difficult to overcome, for the secret of security is in having one's heart fixed on God.

With God, no goal is too lofty to reach—not when you bring the best that you have to the Master, as did the boy with the loaves and fishes—and trust the Lord with the results.

With God, no burden is too heavy to bear, for always underneath are the everlasting arms, lifting us and our burden.

With God, no problem is too difficult to solve—for "we know that all things work together for good to them that love God, to them who are the called according to His purpose." (Romans 8:28)

In *Real Christianity*, written late in the eighteenth century, the great Christian William Wilberforce looked at the world around him and—as some view the world today—decided it was a grim picture of life coming apart. "But," he said, "my hope for the future is not in armies or navies, nor in rulers or national leaders of government.

"My hope for the world," he continued, "is in my firm belief that the world contains many persons of great faith who love the Lord and continue to live by the gospel of Christ."

In other words, with God you can.

Christmas Story: God at Work

Sometimes what seems unusual and mysterious to us is actually God at work.

A Denver newspaper carried a story which served to prove that "God does work in mysterious ways his wonders to perform."

At a church service one night some weeks before Christmas a good and compassionate man heard about a local family facing a gloomy yuletide season. Heavy medical bills had exhausted all of their funds—they would not even try to have a tree.

The good man and his son were determined to see that they had a Christmas tree. Taking the family pickup, they drove into the Colorado Rockies, but unfortunately, the truck skidded off the icy road and hit a large boulder which shattered the windshield and showered them with glass.

They were not seriously injured, but shaken up and needing assistance they watched 100 cars speed by until finally one stopped.

The driver and his wife got out in the freezing cold, helped move the truck off the road, and then drove the man and his son home, and left without identifying themselves.

Later, just before Christmas, the pastor asked the good member of the church to take a basket of food to the unfortunate family for which he had earlier tried to cut a tree.

He found the house but could hardly speak when the door opened. Standing before him was the same couple who had stopped to help him on the mountain road.

He had persisted in his determination to help someone who had already helped him.

God does work in our lives in mysterious, miraculous ways which cannot be discounted as coincidence.

And life continues to look up because God is at work not only at Christmas, but throughout the year.

Somebody's Watching

It would cause all of us to give closer attention to our words and actions if we remembered that somebody is listening and watching.

In almost a joking manner some say, "Remember, Big Brother is watching."

But it goes deeper than that. God sees, God knows, God hears, God cares.

Furthermore, no one is an island, no one can live unto himself. What we do and say becomes public knowledge.

A few years ago, Roy DeBrand, then a pastor in our state, wrote:

"Poor Louie Witt! He went downtown on November 22, 1963, in Dallas to express his displeasure at the liberal policies of the then-President of the United States, John F. Kennedy.

"But things went wrong. Bad wrong. The President was assassinated.

"Photographs taken at the scene showed Witt waving his umbrella in protest. And for fifteen years, there was much speculation about the mysterious 'umbrella man.'

"Conjecture was that perhaps the umbrella was really a gun, or maybe he was a conspirator signalling a gunman when to fire.

"But, alas, it was only mild-mannered Louie Witt waving in protest. As Witt quashed the conspiracy theories in testimony before the House Assassination Committee, he exclaimed:

"If the *Guinness Book of World Records* had a category for people doing the wrong thing at the wrong time in the wrong place, I would be number one with not even a close runner-up."

May the lesson of Louie Witt remind us that we are responsible for our words and actions. All of them. Jesus declared: "Every idle word that men shall speak, they shall give account thereof in the day of judgement." (Matthew 12:36)

I guess that goes for rash, irresponsible actions as well.

So, be careful what you do and say. Somebody's watching.

Wisdom in Few Words

Much wisdom can be contained in a few words.

Here are some well-known words that say much.

Let sleeping dogs lie. (This is good advice for those who have difficulty in leaving well enough alone.)

Bad news travels fast. (Especially is this true with the assistance of those who are more than willing to spread evil tidings.)

Charity begins at home. (Sad thing is that for many persons, it stops there.)

Nothing succeeds like success. (This is not always true. In fact, some of God's great servants, who serve in difficult places, have not succeeded with success—but are courageous and committed enough to give their best, and if need be, fail in the effort.)

In God we trust. (It is unfortunate that although these words are inscribed on U.S. money, the words are not yet written across our hearts and lives.)

But the greatest wisdom is found in these words: Love, repentance, forgiveness, and salvation.

As John 3:16 affirms for all: "God so loved the world that He gave His only begotten Son that whosoever believeth in Him should not perish but have everlasting life."

Faith is reflected in other words of eternal significance:

"Man proposes, God disposes." It is reassuring in our present day to be reminded of a truth we should not forget: God is still in charge and in control. Man proposes, but God disposes.

Finally, there are these words that lift the troubled heart: "This, too, shall pass." Among the most comforting words from Scripture are these: "It came to pass."

Disaster, heartbreak, disappointment, despair—these things did not come to stay. In God's great mercy and love, they came to pass.

Total Love Means Total Acceptance

In fulfilling its useful purpose, Valentine's Day ought to remind us that love is far more than a word in a greeting card.

A moving story is told of a man who finally gathered all of his courage about him and decided to ask his boss for a raise in salary.

On Friday morning at breakfast, he told his wife what he planned to do. All morning at the office he felt nervous and apprehensive. Late in the afternoon, he got up from his desk, stood tall, braced himself, and approached his employer with a request for a much-needed raise.

To his surprise and delight, the boss said, "Yes, I think we can manage that. It will be included in your next paycheck."

He could hardly wait to get home and tell his wife the good news. But when he walked into his house, he saw a beautiful table set with their best dishes.

Candles were lighted. His wife had prepared a wonderful meal! Immediately he surmised that someone from the office had tipped her off!

Finding his wife in the kitchen, he told her the good news. They hugged and kissed, then sat down to the delicious meal.

Next to his plate, the man found a beautiful note: "Congratulations, darling! I knew you'd get the raise! All of this tells you how much I love you."

But while on her way to the kitchen to get dessert, he noticed that a second card had slipped from her pocket. Picking it up, he read: "Don't worry about not getting the raise! You deserve it anyway! These things will tell you how much I love you."

Total love means total acceptance. Her love for him was not dependent upon his success at work.

Even though he failed there and was rejected by his boss, he would be all the more loved and accepted by his wife.

She would stand with him, no matter what, believing in him and loving him.

And that's love to the highest degree. In fact, it is the Christian kind of love.

Voice and Light in the Storm

If we have ears to hear, there are moving words spoken in our Sunday School and church experiences.

Recently, I heard a friend lead in prayer with these words: "Even in the midst of all the lightning and thunder of life, help us to hear the still, small voice of God."

Admittedly, in this troubled day, we do have a great deal of thunder and lightning. In fact, we often have more thunder than lightning—when what we actually need is more light and less noise.

For example, we need more light of concern and compassion and less noise that indicates indifference.

We need the light of understanding and less of the noise of discord.

We need the light of reconciliation and less of the noise of bickering.

We need the light of forgiveness and less noise of fault-finding and judgment.

We need the welcome light of seeking to do what is right rather than adding to the loud noise of wrongdoing.

As my friend said in his prayer, we need to hear the still, small voice of God in the storms of life.

In this deafening age, when there is so much "noise" that is hardly worth hearing, there are some who would say that there is no good noise.

But let us take courage in the fact that there is good news—the good news of the Gospel of Christ.

He is the Voice and the Light in the storm. The chorus of the old hymn says it well:

I've seen it in the lightning,
   heard it in the thunder,
     and felt it in the rain;
My Lord is near me all the time,
   my Lord is near me all the time.

Not Bigger but Fuller Years

In a "Peanuts" comic strip, Lucy says to Charlie Brown, "The years go by too fast—we need bigger years."

This could express the sentiments of many persons as they watch the years go by.

"Where does the time go?" is a question often asked but seldom, if ever, satisfactorily answered.

Still, for all the Lucys who have yearned for "bigger years," truth is, the nature of the universe commands that we shall never have larger years.

In fact, the only option for each of us is that we seek to make better use of the years we have.

Establishing priorities and wisely using our years will enable us to enjoy useful lives in whatever may be the time frame of our existence on earth.

Recognizing a sense of urgency in time usage—as we hear Jesus say, "Work, for the night cometh when no man works"—brings our priorities into sharp focus.

Don't deceive yourself by thinking that you will ever find the time for some great project—take time and carry the project through to a successful conclusion.

Here, then, is a list of priority items for which you should take time.

Take time to pray—it is the language of the soul.

Take time to witness for Christ—if that lost person does not hear of Jesus from you, he may never hear the good news.

Take time to serve—Jesus said, "The greatest among you shall be the servant of all."

Take time to give—"Remember how our Lord said, 'It is more blessed to give than to receive'."

And it all comes down to this truth: The Master would desire for us not "bigger" years, but fuller years.

Humpty Dumpty Wasn't Pushed

The beginning of the new school year brought the usual number of reported classroom antics and amusing incidents.

A television commentator, describing a recent visit to a grammar-school class, said that he was surprised to see on the blackboard a childish scrawl that revealed to the world this startling news: "Humpty Dumpty Was Pushed!"

As every lover of nursery rhymes would agree, this certainly offers one strong explanation of why, when Humpty Dumpty sat on a wall, Humpty Dumpty had a great fall.

But to say he was "pushed" might be stretching the truth a bit. In fact, if you would be kind enough to pardon the pun, I should imagine that all the in-the-know folks would classify this shocking proclamation as nothing more than an "off-the-wall" comment.

However, there is a truth to be learned here concerning an attitude that may be responsible for much of the world's woe.

I refer to the tendency of some to blame every misfortune that comes their way on someone else.

Humpty Dumpty notwithstanding, we are not always "pushed" into our problems. Fact is, we usually fall off the walls of life on our own.

And that is the reason that all the king's horses and all the king's men cannot put Humpty Dumpty or us back together again.

For when we suffer a great fall and life shatters into pieces, it takes the mightiest force in all the world to put it all back together again.

Indeed, it takes the Savior, Christ Jesus, our Lord.

For as the Scripture declares: "And He that sat upon the throne said, 'Behold, I make all things new.' . . . " (Revelation 21:5)

Bake a Friendship Cake

Some years ago there was a popular song entitled "If I'd-a Known You Was Coming, I'd-a Baked a Cake."

The song had a light and bouncy lilt to it, and the words weren't too bad. At least they had a friendly tone.

The old song came to mind when I came across this recipe for a "Friendship Cake":

1 heaping cupful of love
1 handful of forgiveness
1 teaspoon of good humor
a dash of hope
a full pound of unselfishness

1. Set your heart at warm temperature. Mix ingredients smoothly with complete faith in God.

2. Scrape the bowl thoroughly because the great joy of life is often found at the bottom.

3. Spread with tenderness and sprinkle with sympathy and Christian lovingkindness.

4. Cut in large, generous slices. More goodness may be found underneath than is shown on the surface.

5. Serve with a smile, love, and hospitality in a large dish of compassion and understanding.

Offer this cake to your neighbor. In fact, offer it to one and all.

In this kind of recipe, the yield is enough for everyone.

So, try baking a cake and giving it away.

As always, you'll discover that you cannot give away all of any love cake.

For the truth is, the more love you give, the more love you receive.

Pendulating

I am not in agreement with the fellow who said: "I don't enjoy reading the dictionary—it changes the subject too often."

The study of words continues to be fascinating. Some time ago, I came across the word "pendulate" which, according to the dictionary, means "to swing to and fro—as a pendulum."

This seems to be a very appropriate word for today, inasmuch as "pendulating" is the position, or nonposition, of so many.

The Scripture speaks to this: "And Elijah came unto all the people, and said, 'How long halt ye between two opinions? If the Lord be God, follow Him.' . . . " (1 Kings 18:21)

If not the favorite sport, vacillating is certainly a popular pastime with many persons who shift back and forth between two courses of action.

There are those who pendulate between right and wrong, selfishness and generosity, and joy and sadness.

I read of the well-known pastor of a large urban church who stopped to chat with a long-time member of his congregation.

"Well, sister," he asked, "how are you getting along?"

"It's like this, pastor," she replied, "I find myself living somewhere between 'thank you, Lord' and 'help me, Jesus'."

Others could identify with this statement since, for them, life is a series of ups and downs.

But there is a solution that was offered a long time ago by our Lord Who said: "Cheer up—I have overcome the world."

Moreover, there is a need for all of us to follow the example of the apostle Paul who charted his course through many a stormy way with courage born of great faith and commitment.

He lived out before men these brave words: "I can do all things through Christ who strengthens me." (Philippians 4:13)

"Pendulating" and "vacillating" one's way through life can never compare with the victory that comes to those who turn from shaking on the premises to the joy of standing on the promises.

What Are You Doing Now?

Reading somewhere, I came across an account of an unusual tombstone in a distant state and city that had been placed there for a man who was still living.

Chiseled on the stone was the name of the man, date of birth, and a blank space for his future date of death.

The epitaph read: "He bowled 300 in 1962."

This is not to take anything away from the one-time feat of bowling a perfect game—but is this to be his only record of service?

It brings up the question: What do we want to be remembered for? Have we made any lasting contributions to the work of God and the worth of mankind?

Or could it be that some of us are content to rest on our laurels and recline on past achievements.

Ask yourself this question: What have I done since 1962 for the work and witness of Christ?

We can add another thought to the saying

For of all sad words of tongue or pen,
The saddest are these: "It might have been."

We can add:

And still other sad words you see
Are ones that say: "It used to be."

Tears drop from these words:

"They used to be active in the church."
"At one time, he was a deacon."
"She used to be one of our finest Sunday school teachers."

It all comes down to this: What have you done lately for the Lord and His church? What are you doing now?

To have been faithful is one thing—but to continue to be faithful is the main thing.

For those servants of God who persevere and endure may have a blessed tribute inscribed on their tombstones many years from now that reads: "Well done, thou good and faithful servant."

Take Love on the Trip

It is one thing to profess great love, but it is quite another thing to live out that love before all people.

In light of some of the tensions of our day, one wonders how often and in how many gatherings it would have been possible to declare, "See, how these Christians love one another!"

Obviously, love by definition means different things to different people. But, if nothing else, love means to be willing to take the risk that always goes with loving.

As you recall, Jesus said, "If you love me, you will keep my commandments."

And a bit later, in the Gospel of John, we read the words: "A new commandment I give to you that you love one another, even as I have loved you, that you also love one another." (John 13:34)

There is further indication that our Lord considered this as the measurement by which we weigh our true identity as Christians.

Our Lord said as much: "By this all men will know that you are my disciples, if you have love for one another." (John 13:35)

That pretty well says it all. Love is not something you say. It is something you do.

A pastor tells of his friendship with an older minister who was then in his eighties. Because of his failing eyesight, the older man had ridden to a meeting with his young friend, and now they sat for a moment talking in the driveway before going their separate ways.

They talked of their churches, the differences, and the tragedy of the divisions among them. As the old veteran pastor got out of the car, he turned and said: "I may not live to see it, but trust me, the day will come when the church will be known as the people who love each other."

As we travel through life, let us be certain that we take along love. If not, we shall be guilty of leaving out what is most important and essential to the success of any journey.

Adding Flavor to Life

Some are prone to overlook the fact that Christianity is never intended as a killjoy, but a giver of joy.

Christianity is not a subtraction, but an addition to life.

This is something of what the head of a seminary speech department was getting at when a student had read a passage of Scripture, and his comment was: "You preachers can add more black crepe on good news than anyone I have ever seen."

Oliver Wendell Holmes was speaking in the same vein when he commented: "I might have entered the ministry if certain clergymen I knew had not looked and acted so much like undertakers."

Of course, faithful preachers must deal with reality, even though it may not always be pleasant to do so. There is no looking at life through rose-colored glasses.

The Christian gospel does not permit one the luxury of hiding his head in the sand of unreality—ignoring the unpleasant and the difficult.

Jesus told his followers that there is no turning away from the grim realities of life, but that victory is to be won in the presence of them.

As He expressed it: "In the world you shall have tribulation, but be of good cheer, for I have overcome the world."

Knowing this, the Christian can bring joy, zest, and hope to any situation.

Veteran missionary E. Stanley Jones said: "Christianity not only saves you from sin, but from cynicism."

If, as Jesus said, Christians are the salt of the earth, then more of us should be determined to improve the flavor of life by adding the zest of joy.

Make Church Interesting to Keep Worshipers Awake

In speaking to a Models of Metropolitan Ministry Conference, Lyle Schaller, noted church growth authority and parish consultant, indicated that the churches that succeed in today's world will do so by making church interesting and exciting.

Schaller said: "Today folks want worshiping to be interesting."

And, of course, it is obvious that this also applies to preaching.

"Television has radically changed the attitudes of people," Schaller added, "operating under the assumption that it is up to whoever is talking to grab your attention and hold it."

All wives please take note of this startling declaration—especially the wives who in church services have used their elbows to nudge their husbands out of deep slumber.

The expert says it is the responsibility of the speaker to keep worshipers awake.

This is a far cry from the early colonial churches, bowing to the inevitable, by instructing ushers to use a long pole with a hard knob to awaken the sleeping men and boys and a tickling feather to do the same for the women and girls.

Now the new approach for the church program is to have enough sharpness to wake up the slumbering and enough good humor to tickle the pew occupants without a feather.

Of course, we preachers should have suspected that it was our responsibility to keep the congregation awake when a news service reported that a preacher had cured his insomnia by listening to a tape of his Sunday morning messages.

Dullness ought to be listed among the "deadly sins" for preachers.

This scene could have unfolded in AnyChurch, USA.

The preacher was in the midst of his Sunday morning sermon when he spotted a sleeper who was snoring joyfully and noisily.

"Deacon," said the pastor, "wake up Brother Jones!"

Said the deacon to the pastor: "You wake him up—you put him to sleep!"

Looking for Somebody

Serving as a pastor for more than twenty-five years, I spent a considerable amount of time—as did my fellow ministers—looking for the elusive "somebody."

Pastors and other staff members of local churches will immediately know what I mean.

You know that hard-to-find "somebody." When the nominating committee begins the difficult task of trying to enlist people to fill the various places of responsibility in the church, the answer so often received goes like this: "Let somebody else do it!"

The problem is finding that certain "somebody."

Surely, *somebody* can do it. But where is that somebody?

This brings to mind a story about four people named Everybody, Somebody, Anybody, and Nobody.

There was an important job to be done, and Everybody was sure that Somebody would do it.

Oh, Anybody could have done it, but Nobody did it.

Somebody got angry about that, because it was Everybody's job.

Everybody thought that Anybody could do it, but Nobody realized that Everybody wouldn't do it. As you might imagine, it ended up that Everybody blamed Somebody when Nobody did what Anybody could have done.

Too often we attempt to transfer our responsibility to somebody, but the truth is, God has a task for everybody.

Silence Is Golden . . . and Scarce

It will surprise no one to report that the obvious reason talk is so cheap is that the supply always exceeds the demand.

In this day and time, when talkers and talkathons are so prevalent, we must readily admit that silence is not only golden, but very scarce.

One cannot help but wonder just how much better things might be if we all resolved to talk less and pray more.

Remember that wonderful admonition: "If you must whisper, whisper a prayer."

For too long now, many have declared open season on rhetoric.

I recall some years ago hearing one man say of another: "He is outspoken all right, but not by anybody I know of!"

There is a vast difference between being well spoken and outspoken.

In my reading one day, I came across a rule of conduct followed by officers of the British navy. The regulations stated that no naval officer was to be found saying a discouraging word to a fellow officer.

This is excellent advice. Think of it—no more discouraging words spoken to our fellow passengers on the ship of life!

The result of such a practice would be marvelous.

Let's be done with idle, foolish talk. Truth is, when it comes to "capital punishment," let it be clearly understood that it is a terrible death to die—death by elocution.

We would all do well to heed this good advice: Do not speak unless you can improve on the silence.

Mother the Greatest Teacher

The renowned painter Benjamin West gave his mother all of the credit for setting his feet on the pathway to fame.

He recalled an incident from his early childhood when he and his sister were alone one afternoon. With his mother away, little Benjamin thought it would be an ideal opportunity to explore new endeavors.

To his delight, he discovered a large supply of colored ink and decided right then and there to become an artist.

He posed his sister, Sally, as his first subject for a portrait. When his mother came home, boy Benjamin had almost repainted the entire kitchen along with his masterpiece.

Confronted with this disaster, some parents might have flown into a rage. But not his mother. Ignoring the mess, she said, "Why, that's a portrait of Sally!" Then she leaned down to kiss her son.

Said Benjamin West: "My mother's kiss that day made me a painter."

Others join in expressing appreciation for the contribution their mothers made to their lives.

Thomas Edison said, "My mother was the making of me. She was so true, so sure of me, I felt I had someone to live for; someone I must not disappoint."

A London editor submitted to Winston Churchill a list of people who had been his teachers. Churchill returned the list with this comment: "You omitted the greatest of my teachers—my mother."

This is particularly true in the spiritual realm. Richard Cecil, a noted minister, said that when he was a youth he tried his utmost to be an infidel, but his mother's eloquent and beautiful Christian testimony was too much for him.

As a little boy said when told it is God who makes people good, "Yes, I know it is God, but mothers help a lot."

Easing the Struggle

These are strange and unusual times.

Take, for example, the case of the lady who asked her minister if he would please hasten to speak to a member of the congregation who snored very loudly during every service.

However, the minister was a practical man.

"Oh, ma'am, I can't do that," the minister replied.

"Why not?" asked the lady.

"Because he's very valuable to me," said the minister. "He's rendering a real service. His snoring keeps everybody else awake."

Suffice it to say that you can't always tell when someone is making a contribution in an unusual way.

But as a general rule, there are even more persons who, even though they are convinced they are proving to be a great help, are actually a hindrance.

Instead of easing the struggle, they are adding to the struggle.

Two boys on a bicycle built for two had a difficult time climbing a steep hill.

When they finally reached the top, both were near exhaustion, especially the boy in front, who exclaimed: "Whew, I thought we would never make it!"

"Yeah, and we wouldn't have," replied the other, "if I hadn't kept my foot on the brake to keep us from rolling down the hill."

Sort of reminds me of some church members I know—even some Baptists, as a matter of fact.

They think they are helping—but they are hindering the forward progress of the church.

They are applying the brake when they should be applying muscle to the pedal.

What about you? Is the work going forward or being held back because of you?

Are you easing the struggle or adding to the uphill struggle?

It is a good question, and one that only you can answer.

Slow Me Down, Lord

I am certain that many of us would do well to absorb words of that wise old crossroads-store philosopher who said:

"It really doesn't pay to be in too much of a hurry—you just run past more than you catch up with."

In this hectic time in which we live, this is a lesson that is difficult to follow. There is so much to do and so little time in which to do it. There are many miles to travel, many places to go and tasks to bring to completion.

Knowing the fruitlessness of frenzy, the psalmist has said, "Be still and know that I am God."

To be still and recognize the power and greatness of God is the starting place, and we can continue in the right way by heeding prayer thoughts of the unknown author who said:

"Slow me down, Lord.

Ease the pounding of my heart by the quieting of my mind.

Steady my hurried pace with a vision of the eternal reach of time.

Give us, amidst the confusion of the day, the calmness of the everlasting hills.

Break the tension of my nerves with the soothing music of the singing streams that live in my memory.

Teach me the art of taking minute vacations, of slowing down to look at a flower, to chat with a friend, to pat a dog, to read a few lines from the Good Book.

Remind me each day, O Lord, that the race is not always to the swift—and that there is more to life than increasing its speed."

The Big "A"

Lloyd Douglas wrote of an old man he used to visit who taught violin lessons.

One morning Douglas dropped in for a visit and in the course of the conversation said, "Well, what's the good news today?"

Putting his violin aside, the old man stepped over to a tuning fork suspended from the ceiling by a silk cord. Taking a small mallet in hand, he struck the tuning fork a sharp blow and said:

"There is good news today. That, my friend, is 'A.' It was 'A' all day yesterday. It will be 'A' all day tomorrow, all next week, all next month, and even for a thousand years."

Continuing, the violinist said: "The soprano upstairs screeches off key, the tenor down the hall flats his high notes, and the piano across the hall is way out of tune. There is so much noise all around me, but that, my friend," striking the tuning fork again, "is 'A'."

This is a stupendous truth that can put iron into spiritually tired blood.

The truth is this: No matter how much the world may get out of tune, no matter how much discord fills the air, some things are fixed. They abide.

Faith, hope, love—these three abide—but the greatest of these is love. That's a big "A."

Other things may fall away and crumble to dust at our feet, but the big "A" verse of the Bible remains ever and always in tune: "For God so loved the world, that he gave his only begotten Son, that whosoever believeth in him should not perish, but have everlasting life."

That's the big "A" of affirmation—that's the big "A" of assurance—and that's the big "A" that is always in tune with the needs of all mankind.

Wanted: Maturity

One of the great problems adding to the difficulties of those who honestly desire to be God's people is the glaring lack of maturity.

I believe it was the late R. G. Lee who referred to the problem for some preachers who are expected to preach "sermonettes" for "Christianettes."

Maturity, in the sense that we strive to be those who practice exemplary Christian conduct, would go a long way toward solving problems in church and out of church.

Speaking of immaturity, the way in which some speak shows a lack of maturity. For example, there is the perennial "Pop-off."

You don't have to ask him. He will tell you anyway. Taking pride in the fact that he always "shoots from the lip," he usually leaves injured people and projects in his pathway. He talks down more than others can talk up.

Then, there is the "Goof-off." He has never matured into a full-grown worker. He is trying harder to get out of work than he is to get into work. His theme is always, "Let somebody else do it." With this attitude, he is a hindrance rather than a help to the Lord's work.

Next, there is the immature "Run-off." If things don't go to suit him, he simply runs off. He is not mature enough to stand and stay and resolve the situation. He prefers to rant and run.

Of all the immature attitudes, perhaps none is more costly to the overall progress of the work than the "Show-off." If he is not the captain of the team, he won't play. If he is not center stage and in the spotlight, he won't perform.

It's puzzling, though, how persons reconcile this attitude with the words of Jesus Who said: "I am among you as one that serveth."

Or even the words of John who said of Jesus: "He must increase, but I must decrease."

Let the want ad read: "WANTED—to meet the needs of our day—this kind of Christian maturity."

The Sounds of Hope

As the story goes, there was a speaker who was notoriously bad about saying he would speak only a certain length of time, and then going on and on.

When he got up before this particular audience, he promised them he would speak only twenty minutes. When he had talked twenty minutes, though, he kept right on going.

He reached the thirty-minute mark, then forty, fifty, and on to an hour. By this time the audience was getting very restless and nervous.

The man who had introduced him was becoming madder by the minute. When he had reached the hour-and-a-half mark, the situation was near the breaking point.

The man who had introduced him was so furious he decided to throw his gavel at him. He threw it with all his strength, but missed the speaker and hit a baldheaded man seated on the front row.

As the man passed into a state of unconsciousness from the blow, he cried out in a loud voice, "Hit me again—I'm still hearing him!"

There may be many persons who would like to shut out certain irritating sounds in this troubled day.

In this mixed-up world, there are many disturbing sounds and events that perplex us. As one publication said, "Perhaps the hardest thing to do now is to develop a proper balance between gloom and hope."

Well, for the Christian, the balance lies in looking to Jesus Who is "the same yesterday, today, and forever."

One is able to rise above circumstances when he can join in singing the old hymn: "My hope is built on nothing less than Jesus' blood and righteousness."

This is balancing hope over against gloom. And come what may, this is the solid rock on which we can stand.

Timid or Expectant Prayers?

Prayer, in the highest sense, depends upon the perception of faith of the one who prays.

Hebrews 11:6 declares, "for he who comes to God must believe that He is, and that He is a rewarder of those who seek Him." (NASB)

Many of us who go to God with our prayers resemble the timid door-to-door salesman who knocks on the door, steps back, and says: "I hope nobody is home—I hope, I hope, I hope."

Some would-be practitioners of prayer are like the little girl who came by the house to sell magazines. When the door opened, she said, "I don't suppose you want to buy any magazines, do you?"

God does not answer such prayers. God answers prayers that are spoken with expectancy by a Christian who believes that God is and that He is the rewarder of those who diligently seek Him.

Marianne Adlard, a bedridden girl in London, read of the work of Dwight L. Moody among the ragged children of Chicago and began to pray, "O, Lord, send this man to our church."

In 1872, Dr. Moody took his second trip to London for an intended rest. However, when the pastor of Marianne's church met him and asked him to preach, Dr. Moody agreed.

At the close of the service, Dr. Moody asked if anyone wanted to receive Christ, and dozens came forward. Dr. Moody preached again and continued to preach for ten days, with 400 conversions.

Wanting to know the explanation for the extraordinary movement of the Spirit, Dr. Moody found a bedridden girl praying that God would bring him to her church.

"God heard her and brought me over 4,000 miles of land and sea at her request."

Faithful prayer with great expectation brings great results.

Easter Comes Again and None Too Soon

Easter, like springtime, arrives; and it is even more warmly welcomed than the changing of the seasons.

Easter comes in God's own good time frame, and none too soon. Until that first glad resurrection day, the world had walked under the cloud of death.

The cold winter of mortality had gripped the earth and all of its people, and then Christ arose!

Something happened in that event that made Christ more alive on the streets of Jerusalem forty days after his crucifixion than on the day of his triumphal entry.

Even modern man must recognize that if Easter means anything, it means that eternal truth is eternal.

You may nail it to a cruel tree, wrap it up in grave clothes and seal it in a tomb; but "truth crushed to earth, shall rise again."

Truth does not perish. It cannot be destroyed. It may be distorted, or even silenced temporarily.

It has been compelled to carry its cross to Calvary's hill, but, with an inevitable certainty, after Black Friday dawns truth's Easter morning.

We need to know again in our hearts the reality of the risen Christ.

Weary and worn, sad and forlorn, disturbed and discouraged with life's trivial tune? Listen, there's the glorious sound of the stone rolling away from the tomb.

Once more there is before us the risen Christ.

Easter comes again, and none too soon.

Arrested for Bad Singing!

A news item reported that a Texas church had obtained a restraining order against a woman for loudly singing off key and "disturbing the worship services."

She was arrested after failing to attend a hearing on the order.

To my knowledge, there has been no word of such disputes since the congregation and choir of a church in Oak Creek, Wisconsin, were warned by authorities to sing more quietly or be faced with a fine.

As I recall, at the time there was a rather heated disagreement as to whether they were "making a joyful noise," as the Bible says, or "just an awful noise," as the complaint said.

This situation reminds me of the announcement in a church bulletin: "Our mixed chorus sang last Sunday in a regional broadcast from Minneapolis. It was nice to hear them and realize they were nearly 1,000 miles away."

But, still, the act of arresting a woman for loudly singing off key seems a bit harsh.

Heretofore, such annoying voices prompted nothing more serious than the erroneous congregational assumption that something was either terribly wrong with the music program or the organ was in need of tuning, and, if the congregation felt musically disturbed, it was only because some voices gave the impression that the singers were actually yelling for help.

But in this incident from Texas, certain other considerations come to mind. Did the restraining order allow the woman the privilege of moving her lips—though uttering no sound?

But there is a greater concern for all of us who belong to the discordant detachment. If they arrested everyone in all churches who sing off key, we might have more members in jail than we have in church.

Enthusiasm and Success

Charles M. Schwab, who started in the steel industry with a surveying crew at one dollar a day and ended up as chairman of the board of Bethlehem Steel, said, "A man can succeed at anything for which he has enthusiasm."

The sense of this word among the Greeks affords the noblest definition of it: *enthusiasm* signifies "God in us."

And to turn the phrase around, with "God in us" we ought to be enthusiastic.

Obviously, one of the great needs of our time is a weapon to fight apathy. And here it is: God-inspired enthusiasm.

So many persons, with empty lives, have the pessimistic attitude that declares, "I couldn't care less."

But compare lives of this emotionally empty crowd with lives of individuals who approach life—even its rough moments—with confidence, hope, faith, and enthusiasm.

One need not ask who lives the fuller life—or who accomplishes most?

As Emerson said, "Every great and commanding movement in the annals of the world is the triumph of enthusiasm. Nothing great was ever achieved without it."

Enthusiasm joined to a great Christian faith lifts life out of the ordinary, makes it mean something—something above and beyond itself.

Charles Kingsley declared, "We act as though comfort and luxury were the chief requirements of life, but not so. All that we need to make us really happy is something to be enthusiastic about."

And if God is in us, we have that which brings purpose and power to our lives.

We can then look up—with enthusiasm.

At Peace with Everyone

"If it be possible, as much as lieth in you, live peaceably with all men." (Romans 12:18)

This is a tall order—even for a Christian—but it is an utter impossibility for the non-Christian.

I heard once of a five-year-old whom a teacher found with clinched fists in the corner of a kindergarten.

"What are you doing?" the teacher inquired.

"I'm learning not to hit," explained the youngster.

It is good for all—the five-year-olds and older—to learn to keep from hitting other people.

But the Christian standard goes deeper and higher than that. Christians must learn not to want to hit!

To reach that lofty standard, our hearts must be so full of love for our fellowman that it washes away all the sore spots.

That reminds me of the incident that took place one day when Sleepy Meanwell was standing in front of the crossroads store talking to Cy Downflap, when Cy's dog Elijah started chasing a pickup truck.

Elijah had engaged in car chasing for several years and had been reasonably successful at it, but on this occasion his timing was off. He got his teeth caught in a rear tire and flew through the air, hitting Sleepy Meanwell in the chest.

The dog got up, shook himself, bit Sleepy on the foot, and ran growling and whimpering under the porch of the store.

Elijah never could stand Sleepy after that. From Elijah's point of view, Sleepy had kicked the daylights out of him.

There's a truth here: Many of our enemies are folks we collided with when we ran into something too big to handle.

So let's seek to live peaceably with all men—it results in a more pleasant trip down the road of life.

Don't Miss the Splendor

Life as we know it is so filled with distractions that it is possible to live a lifetime and yet miss the big event.

It's like the country boy who was given money by his father so he could attend his first circus.

In eager anticipation, the boy ran off for town. As he arrived, the crowd was gathering for the passing circus parade. Wide-eyed and amazed at what he saw, he stood, watched the parade, and then handed his ticket money to the last clown in the procession.

Like so many, he had seen the parade—but missed the big event.

In the child's story, the cat who went to London to visit the queen was so distracted in chasing a mouse under the queen's chair that she missed the splendor of the court and the sight of the queen.

So it is that we often become so distracted by insignificant things that we lose sight of or never really see the splendor of the Lord.

This is often true in a worship experience. At the very time and place when we ought to behold God's glory and enlarge our hearts, we become distracted with lesser things.

As someone has said, "Satan would have the would-be worshiper keep his mind on little things: 'The usher is a hypocrite' . . . 'The woman in the opposite pew couldn't dress so nicely if she paid her debts'."

The idea of Satan is to never let the worshiper see the church with the cross held high because that is a sight at which all hell trembles.

Satan is the great distracter. "Don't listen to the preacher expounding God's Word. Turn toward the crying baby. Watch as someone leaves the auditorium."

Enter into every distraction, and you will see everything but the Lord's splendor.

And Satan would also turn us to side issues—leading us to exchange the eternal for the trivial and the essential for the nonessential.

Let us make certain we do not allow distractions to detour and deter us from doing the work to which God has called us.

Don't mistake the parade for the big event. Don't miss the splendor!

Heads in the Church

A Methodist preacher wrote a column in a county newspaper on the interesting subject of "Heads in the Church."

Identifying himself as "The Circuit Rider," the minister suggested the following "church heads."

(1) *Figureheads.* Easy to recognize in most any church, the figure-heads are glad to accept the glory and reject the work. They are happy to assume authority—so long as others carry the load.

(2) *Soreheads.* They are easy to spot. They wear a frown most of the time. They are sore about everything. Nothing pleases them—but they are not going to say anything about it—except to everyone they meet.

(3) *Deadheads.* No need to ask them. They are not going to do anything. Their theme is always same song, second verse: "Why don't you get someone else to do it?" And although you may seek in every way to enlist them in the service of the church—you may even beg a lot—their response is always the same: "I'd rather not!" Truth is, they "retired" from everything a good many years ago. They just never got around to announcing it.

(4) *Hotheads.* Rub them the wrong way, and you can readily identify the hotheads in any crowd. They have a short fuse. It is a wonder they have any temper left—they've lost it so many times. Their favorite expression is: "I really told him or them off." And their favorite sport is jumping at conclusions.

But there is another head in the church of which Jesus spoke with much appreciation.

In fact, Jesus showed us the way, "taking upon Himself the form of a servant."

A *Head Servant* within the church has blessed the work through the ages and shall continue to be a blessing until time is no more.

Jesus said it: "The greatest among you shall be the servant of all."

Unapologetically Christian

An outstanding corporation president had been asked to speak to a group of businessmen on his successful operation.

He told his host, "Well, I will have to tell them we operate on Christian principles."

"You can't say that," he was told, "because there will be Buddhists and other non-Christians here."

He answered, "If you can't let me tell about the principles by which we operate, I will not speak."

He spoke, and Buddhists and other non-Christians came up to commend him on his presentation and the principles upon which he operated.

Why should we be two-faced and apologetic about being a Christian? For fear of offending non-Christians in public gatherings, some Christians are reluctant to pray in Christ's name.

At commencement exercises, I understand, the prayer is now offered "in the name of the Great Educator."

What is often overlooked is the fact that some Christians in attendance are offended by this obvious cop-out.

Supposedly, if this trend continues, and invocations are permitted, we shall hear prayers being offered at sports events "in the name of the Great Scorekeeper."

This brings into sharp focus one of the problems in our day, namely, our growing lack of consistency in our Christian walk and testimony.

If we are Christians in church, why not be Christian in the marketplace?

If we are Christians in the pulpit, why not be Christian when praying from the public platform?

Let us mean what we say and say what we mean.

Let us live who we are and what we are before all men in all places.

And this is my prayer—in Jesus' name.

God's Bigger Shovel

Some people seem to be reluctant to open up with an honest steward-ship of possessions, holding back as if they thought they could outgive God.

It is impossible to outgive God. Fact is, our Heavenly Father always has larger blessings in store for his children who seek to return a just portion of all that they receive.

As one wise old man told me, "It's not all right to talk about giving something to God. You see, God owns it all, anyway."

The story has it that a certain well-to-do farmer was widely known for his generous giving to his church.

His reputation as a good steward and strong supporter of his local church in all missions causes spread throughout the entire community.

Friends and acquaintances were puzzled as to how this man could give so much away and yet continue to be so prosperous.

One day, a friend stopped the generous steward on the street and said, "I just can't stand it any longer. I have to know. We simply can't understand you. We know you give far more than the rest of us and yet remain so wealthy."

The farmer said, "It's no secret."

"Well, then, tell us," his friend insisted, "you make tremendous contributions and yet you always seem to have more to give."

"Oh," the farmer declared, "that is easy to explain. I keep shoveling into God's bin, and God keeps shoveling into mine—but God has the bigger shovel!"

There is another way to say it: He that soweth sparingly shall reap sparingly, but he that soweth bountifully shall reap bountifully.

That's the way of God's big shovel!

More in the Window than on the Shelf

I vividly recall an illustration used by a forceful and effective preacher who stood once before a display window of a downtown shoe store and sighted a pair of shoes that was "just what he wanted."

Going inside the store, he found a salesperson and told him that he wanted a pair of shoes exactly like those in the display window.

"Come and show me which shoes you mean," the salesclerk said.

Going outside, the pastor pointed to the shoes of his choice and said, "There—right there—that's the pair I want to buy."

"Oh," said the salesclerk, "I'm sorry—we do not have those shoes in stock."

"You mean," said the pastor, "you have shoes on display but you do not have them inside the store!"

"Yes," said the clerk, directing the would-be customer to a small printed sign with the words "All Shoes on Display in the Window May Not Be on the Inside."

What a commentary on our time in which we live. Think of it: all that we see on display may not be on the inside.

I can remember the comment of a great and wise old Christian professor who was once asked to give his assessment of the true ability of a preacher who had soared into the spotlight of wide acclaim and achieved what seemed to be instant success. Reflecting for just a moment, this perceptive old man of God said, "He's got more in the window than he's got on the shelf."

The world looks on the outside, but "God looketh on the heart of man."

It is a lesson in truth needed by all of us. May our Christian dedication be consistent with what we put on display.

And then, it could be said of more of us: "What you see on the outside is what you find on the inside."

True Leadership

I was glad to have the informative and inspiring experience of attending a Congress on Leadership.

The addresses by all the speakers were outstanding, with everyone coming to the plate and hitting a home run.

One speaker I remember in particular shared the method he used in research on his address on leadership as being a bit unorthodox, but effective.

Going to the courthouse square in a small Tennessee town, he interviewed some of the stalwart citizens holding forth on a bench there.

"What is a leader?" he asked, as they came up with these interesting answers.

"A leader is one who sees all the dragons but is careful about the ones he chooses to slay."

"A leader is one who sees the big picture but can focus on that one most important thing."

While the research was in progress, a young attorney entered the courthouse, and one old man said, "Now there goes a leader!"

"Why do you consider him a leader?" he was asked.

"Because," was the reply, "he knows something that all the rest of the folks don't know—he knows what he is doing."

One cannot deny that this is a requirement for leadership.

Further research on the definition of leadership brought this classic comment: "A leader is one who knows whose hand is in whose pocket and why."

This goes along with the old saying: "There are two kinds of leaders in the world—some are interested in the fleece—others in the flock."

But it was also pointed out in the conference that Jesus Christ is the model for true leadership. He chose to be a servant—to meet the deepest needs of His followers.

For, in truth, the greatest power Christians can have is the power to serve. Servant leadership is universally applicable—as effective in the executive suite as in our churches and schools.

It is the kind of leadership that never looks down on anyone, but always looks up.

Sound and Fury

National Public Radio reported the Bowes Corporation has developed special antinoise headsets designed to cancel loud noises for helicopter pilots and others afflicted by the noises of their daily work and activities. This ought to be a useful invention, considering the many painful noises presently persecuting the ears of mankind.

For example, all modern-day music cannot be classified as "good and loud"—just loud.

And there are other disturbing voices that cause both the heart and ears to ache: noises of criticism, selfishness, littleness, and hatred.

Someone has said: Speakers who give us much noise and many words and are most loud when least lucid should take a lesson from nature, which often gives lightning without thunder but never thunder without lightning.

To illustrate, I recall a certain preacher who chose as his text "Be still and know that I am God"—and then proceeded to shout it out during his entire message.

Alexander Pope said, "It is with narrow-souled people as with narrow-necked bottles: the less they have in them, the more noise they make in pouring it out." And yet, the caustic, critical, fault-finding noisemaker is perhaps the hardest to take. The biblical writer declared, "The tongue can no man tame." (James 3:8)

Asked by his master to prepare the best dish possible, a servant prepared a dish of tongue, saying, "It is best of all dishes because with it we may bless and communicate happiness, dispel sorrow, remove despair, cheer the fainthearted, inspire the discouraged, and lift up mankind."

Later the servant was asked to prepare the worst dish, and a platter of tongue again appeared on the table. The servant said, "It is the worst, because with it we may break hearts, destroy reputations, promote discord and strife, and set people at war with each other." He was a discerning servant.

Solomon wisely said, "Whoso keepeth his mouth and his tongue keepeth his soul from troubles." (Proverbs 21:23)

Committed to Work

With some, the joy of laboring at one's job is overlooked—even during the observance of Labor Day weekend. Old-timers remind us that many people do not know how to work as they once did. And there is some evidence to support this, as in the case of an efficiency expert interviewing two clerks in a government office in Washington.

"What do you do here?" he asked one. The clerk, offended by the question, growled, "I don't do anything." The interrogator made a note and asked the other man the same question. The second man replied, "I don't do anything, either." The questioner nodded knowingly and said, "A clear case of duplication."

There are those who believe that work does not mix very well with anything. But there are others who have the mistaken idea that business and religion won't mix.

Two friends once formed a partnership to open a butcher shop. The business prospered, and they made good money for many years. One day an evangelist came to town and conducted a revival meeting. The first partner went to church, was converted, born again, and happy about it. Partner One came to work the next morning, shared the good news with Partner Two, encouraging him to give his heart to the Lord also. "Hold on," said Partner Two, "I'm glad you've got religion, but if I'm converted, too, who's going to weigh the meat?"

True commitment is the key. A resort minister who regularly visited each area campsite every week was confronted by a huge growling dog. The vicious-looking dog bared his teeth and moved forward, but since the dog's owner seemed unconcerned, the young pastor took a seat behind the camper for a short visit. As he prepared to leave, the pastor commented upon the ferocious appearance of the dog. The camper agreed and then added: "Yep, he's trained to attack, but he's not very good at it."

Although grateful for the lack of commitment on the dog's part, the young minister was reminded that many church members are like that—well trained and able to serve, but still not active in the Lord's work. The problem of ineffective service is often not so much a lack of training, but of commitment. The dog was trained to attack, but his heart was not in it.

Are our hearts really in the work, or do we just go through reluctant motions? Let us hope it shall *not* be said of us: "They are trained to serve, but they are not very good at it."

The Blessing of Gratitude

It has been said that a good memory is one that can remember the day's blessings and forget the day's troubles.

Certainly this attitude would be most appropriate for observance of Thanksgiving.

We should remember the wonderful blessings that come to us from the hands of our generous and gracious God and forget the irritations that subtract from our happiness.

Unfortunately, the expression of gratitude is not appreciated by all. On Thanksgiving Day, a pastor in Grand Rapids was served papers arresting him for noise pollution and disturbing the peace. His offense: over the loudspeaker in the church tower, he was playing the hymn "Now Thank We All Our God."

According to a city ordinance, he was guilty of creating a general nuisance. Is Thanksgiving ever to be interpreted as a nuisance?

Not if we remember God's gift of life and forget the negatives that needle us.

Gratitude enables us to remember the friends who encourage us and forget the frustrations that discourage us.

We must not forget to remember our blessings. Thanksgiving ought to be a daily part of our lives, a disposition of the soul, an orientation toward God, resulting in an appreciative outlook on life.

Dissatisfaction with life often springs from covetousness and greed. Too many suffer from the malady of unsatisfied greed.   Contentment is not in having everything, but in being satisfied with what God has given us.

Those who are in right relationship with God reflect gratitude as a way of life, and persons who live in daily attitude of gratitude do so because they recognize the goodness and the gifts of God.

This is thanksgiving and thanksliving.

On Top of Circumstances

A young minister, bathing himself in self-pity, was trying to work through some discouraging times in his pastorate. He decided to visit an old and experienced pastor.

Taking his seat, he looked across the desk at this seasoned warrior who had survived many conflicts over the years and always seemed to return to the battle with new vitality and determination.

"Well, it's good to see you," his old friend said, "Tell me, how are things going?"

"Oh," answered the young pastor, "I guess things are going fairly well under the circumstances."

"Under the circumstances, under the circumstances?" shot back the veteran pastor, "What do you mean, under the circumstances? Get on top of the circumstances!"

This is excellent advice. For it is too often true that we find comfort in using pet phrases such as "under the circumstances" when actually we ought to be working harder and get on top of the circumstances.

One other phrase we often use in replying to questions of how things are going is: "Well, pretty good, all things considered."

But the point is, do we ever truly consider all things? Certainly we are prone to consider all problems, difficulties, hardships, hurts, and sorrows.

But have we considered all things? Have we considered that we have a good and loving God Who desires the best for His children?

God loves us with a love that never lets go. Have we considered the grace of God? "His grace is sufficient."

Have we considered the strength of God? "In all these things, we are more than conquerors through Him Who loved us." (And gave Himself for us.)

When we actually and positively "consider all things," then we may well be "more than conquerors," and shall move with all deliberate speed to get on top of our circumstances.

Keep the Light Burning

When the events of our days are chronicled, it shall be said of some: Their creed was *Speed!* Their motto was *Rush!* As someone has said:

This is the age of the half-read page,
And a quick hash and a mad dash,
The plane hop and the brief stop,
The brain strain and the heart pain,
The catnaps 'til the spring snaps--
This is our culture.

The old hymn still offers excellent advice, which should be heeded by all:

Take time to be holy, Speak oft with thy Lord;
Abide in Him always, And feed on His Word;
Make friends of God's children, Help those who are weak;
Forgetting in nothing His blessing to seek.

The suggestions of Henry Van Dyke should help us to keep things in proper perspective:

Remember the weakness and loneliness of people who are growing older.
Stop asking how many of our friends love us and ask ourselves if we love them enough.
Bear in mind the things that other people have to bear on their hearts.
Make a grave for our ugly thoughts and a garden for our friendly feelings, with the gate open.
Trim our lamp so that it will give more light and less smoke, and carry it in front of us so that our shadow will fall behind us.

May we let our light shine, placing it high on a hill for all to see.

For if, as Jesus said, we are "the light of the world," then we need to light the way for our fellowman.

Faith and Tenacity

Among the Baptists of Poland I discovered a number of my kind of folks.

During a good many years in the pastorate and in other work, it has been my feeling that no matter how difficult the task, if you remain together with God and each other, you can—through Christ—do anything.

Apparently, there are many Polish Baptists who preach and practice the same faith.

Facing difficult obstacles with determination and tenacity, they move on through many dangers, toils, and snares until they accomplish their goals.

A good illustration of this is the West Katowice Baptist Church, which we visited one morning on our way to Cracow.

Located in a coal-mining community, this church is now enjoying its first building in its seventy-year history.

Can you imagine waiting seventy years in America for the first church building? We could if we were members of this Polish congregation.

Pastor Stephan Rogaczewski said that twice they had raised the necessary funds for the building, but something happened and they had to start over.

"Our church had no home, no building, not even our own mailing address," the pastor said.

During World War II, when Germany occupied Poland, the building fund was sent to Berlin and lost. But faith continued, and now the church has a beautiful new building costing $103,000.

Some who contributed through the years were not privileged to see the church building. But they must rejoice in heaven.

The church now has 175 members, and in the past three years has baptized forty-two students.

It was appropriate that before saying goodbye to the pastor, our group joined him in singing "Amazing Grace."

Commitment, faith and tenacity will win when nothing else can.

Many Happy Returns

The Christmas season reminds us once again of the joy of giving.

"It is," as Jesus said, "more blessed to give than to receive."

It is an inescapable truth that one who gives more seems to receive more from life.

Even if this does not always hold true from the material sense—it is true from the standpoint of blessings received.

There is the joy that goes with doing something for others, to say nothing of the inner satisfaction of being unselfish.

And giving, in the right spirit and for the right reasons, is a recognition of the fact that you spell "give," l-o-v-e.

Moreover, if the blessing of giving is not enough, we are also privileged to receive many happy returns.

A soldier, stationed at one of our army bases in the United States, was injured in an accidental fire.

Rushed to the base hospital for emergency treatment, he was receiving a blood transfusion when he looked up, and to his astonishment saw that the container carried his name as the donor.

Then, he remembered. A light came on in his mind. The donor was now the recipient!

A few weeks before, the call had gone out for all those who would volunteer to give blood.

He had volunteered. Now, in time of need, he was having returned to him that which he had given.

The lesson here is obvious. Don't be afraid to give. It is a blessing to give.

And the giver shall have many happy returns!

The Art of Forgetting

The merits of having a good memory are lauded by one and all.

Some conduct seminars on ways to improve your memory. Others suggest a daily dose of garlic as a means of adding to one's ability to remember.

This does, I understand, help other people to remember to avoid you!

However, it is true that everyone desires the blessing of a good memory. But in one sense, it could be said that there are benefits in being able to forget.

We would do well to cultivate the art of forgetting—as stated so well in this anonymous prayer:

Lord, please shorten my memory.
I remember some things way too long, Lord.
I remember words of criticism that were spoken so long ago
    the critic can't even remember having said them.
And, Lord, if someone has lied to me or about me,
    I never seem to forget.
I remember when people fail to keep their promises.
And I don't ever seem to forget the selfishness and littleness
    of certain acquaintances and associates.
I remember far too long the gifts I've given to some—
    with nothing received in return.
I never forget when someone "puts me down,"
    and apparently I want to hold on to that resentment.
Lord, please shorten my memory!

Help me to "forget those things that are behind and reach forth unto those things that are before, pressing toward the mark for the prize of the high calling of God in Christ Jesus."

This is a need for most of us: to remember the blessing of forgetting.

The Blessed Hope

A long and thoughtful look at the passing scene shows that persons who seem to "have it all together" are those who at some juncture in their lives have shaken hands with hope.

They do not dwell on the dark side. They look for the sunshine. Their emphasis is not on pessimism but optimism.

No matter what happens, they seem to have a built-in confidence that something good is just around the next bend in the road.

How is it that these people of hope seem to glow and glide through life rather than warring with life?

Experience suggests certain valid reasons. For one thing, they believe in the power of prayer and live in the strength of it.

When trouble comes their way, they talk it over with God. Following the advice of the old hymn, they take their burdens to the Lord and "leave them there."

Then, too, people of hope believe in the goodness of God and His unfailing love for them. They know that they cannot outrun the love of God, for He loves them with a love that will not let them go.

Moreover, people of great hope are always people of great faith. Their optimism does not come from within themselves; it springs from a deep and abiding faith in God.

They have plugged into a source of power above and beyond themselves. And that hope is born of prayer, accentuated by the love of God, and continued in a great faith. And this makes possible the victorious life in spite of obstacles and hardships.

When one great man of God was asked how he managed to remain so triumphant in the midst of extreme difficulty, he answered for all of the people of hope when he said, "I don't let nobody blow no black smoke on my blue skies!"

Letting Them Down Easy

Tactfulness is difficult to find in our day.

There are many individuals who seem to garner satisfaction from "telling them off" rather than tactfully discussing problems with other people.

Too many of us have a bad habit of forgetting the apostle Paul's excellent advice: "Let your speech be always with grace, seasoned with salt, that you may know how you ought to answer every man." (Colossians 4:6)

There are others who pride themselves on being adept at saying the right thing at the right time, but when it comes to the actual situation where tactfulness is sorely needed, they are sadly lacking.

An old story serves to illustrate. In a certain rural area of the state, an unfortunate accident occurred one afternoon at the local sawmill.

A man by the name of Jones was killed. Other workers, shocked by the tragedy, stood around discussing who would receive the hard assignment of telling the wife of Jones.

One fellow, who was always quick of tongue and slow of mind, said he would carry out that assignment.

"But you must be tactful," someone said.

"Don't worry," the man replied, "I will take care of it—I know exactly how to handle it."

He then got in his truck, drove to the house, knocked on the door, and when it opened, he blurted out: "Is this where the Widow Jones lives?"

Bad news is difficult to reveal to those involved. But some few have mastered the art of tactfulness.

Once a friend had to write to the family of his buddy who went afoul of the law in the early days of the Wild West and was sentenced to hang.

After struggling with a way to break the news, he wrote, "It is with deep regret that I must inform you that your son died here while taking part in a public ceremony. The platform on which he was standing gave way."

That's letting them down easy.

Father God's Gift, Too

There is no doubt that one of God's great gifts to His children is a good mother. Equal time is appropriate for fathers, although this is not always freely given.

The muted emphasis on the father's importance can be seen in the question a child asked of his mother: "If the stork brings babies, if Santa Claus brings our presents, if the Lord gives our daily bread and Uncle Sam our Social Security, why do we keep Daddy around?"

That is an interesting question, and so is this: Is a good father a gift from God? I believe the answer is Yes.

But often this appreciation is not readily expressed. Note these letters from children:

> Dear Dad: I don't think my teacher believes in Father's Day, because she just gave me my report card, and it has to be signed today.

> Dear Father: Because it is Father's Day, I am going to promise not to get into any trouble all day—so that is why I am going to sleep all day.

> Dear Dad: I think you are a great father, even if you don't give me a raise in my allowance.

This was pointed out also in a letter from college:

> Dear Dad: You haven't sent me a check in two weeks. What kind of Christian kindness is that?

Letter from home:

> Dear Son: That is known as unremitting Christian kindness.

However, many fathers are like Charles Dickens, who wrote to his son Henry while he was at college, advising him to stay out of debt and confide all his perplexities to his father. The letter concluded:

> I must strongly impress upon you the priceless value of the New Testament, and the study of that book as the one unfailing guide in life.
>
> Bowing down before our Saviour, you cannot go very wrong, and will always preserve at heart a true spirit of humility.
>
> Similarly, I impress upon you the habit of saying a Christian prayer every night and morning. These things have stood by me all through my life. And so will God bless you!

The Greatest Satisfaction

The term "the greatest" is used rather loosely in our day.

One frequently hears someone say, "He is the greatest" or "She is the greatest."

In the world of sports, "greatest" is used as a description of many well-known athletes.

However, I came across a more meaningful list of what is appropriately described as "the greatest," namely, these:

The greatest disturber and disrupter is gossip. Words so easily spoken often do irreparable harm, and injurious words of gossip, once said, are as hard to retrieve as feathers in a windstorm.

The greatest crippler is fear, because it paralyzes.

The greatest mistake is giving up before the mission is completed.

The greatest joy is being needed.

The greatest opportunity is always the next one.

The greatest thought is that of the true and loving God.

The greatest victory is always the victory over self.

The greatest handicap of any life is the sin of selfishness. Egotism has slain its millions.

The greatest loss is the loss of self-confidence. Without self-confidence and, more importantly, a faith that says, "Even if I can't, God can," it is difficult to have the resilience with which to bounce back from a disappointing failure.

The greatest need in life is a living relationship with Jesus Christ.

And the greatest satisfaction in all of life is to seek the will of God, and having found it, to follow it.

Ready for the Trip?

A minister drove into a service station on the start of the Fourth of July weekend and found it to be unusually crowded.

Automobiles were lined up at the gas pumps, and "busy" was too mild a word to describe the attendant.

Finally, after a long wait, the harried and hurried attendant got around to the clergyman who had been waiting a long time.

He apologized, saying, "Seems like everyone waits until the last minute to get ready for a long trip."

The minister smiled and said, "I know what you mean. I have the same problem in my line of work."

And when you come to think of it, this is puzzling. Think of it: when all is said and done, this final journey into eternity is one we must all take.

There are no alternate routes, nor detours. No way to avoid this journey.

Ultimately, this is a trip that all must face.

If nothing else, it ought to alert us to the wisdom of being prepared for the journey.

A favorite aunt, the older sister of my mother, lived to be a ripe old age. Until her later years, she was active, always ready to take a trip.

It was a family joke to say: "She always had her bag packed."

When I assisted in her funeral service, I remarked that, "In the finest sense, her bag was packed; she was ready to go."

And for the Christian who would go to that final heavenly abode, this is the only way to live: bag packed with commitment, dedication, and faith that our Lord has gone to prepare a place which shall be ready for us at the end of life's journey.

Are you ready for the trip?

The Right Viewpoint

Two small boys were at play, when an interesting conversation took place.

"Wouldn't you hate to wear glasses all the time?" asked one boy of his playmate.

"No," answered the playmate slowly, "Not if I had my Grandma's kind of glasses. She sees how to fix a lot of things, and sees a lot of exciting things to do on rainy days."

"Grandma's glasses are unusual all right," he continued. "She has a neat way of seeing when folks are really tired and worried, and she always sees what will help everybody and make them feel better.

"With her glasses, Grandma always sees what you meant to do—even if you don't do things just right.

"I asked her one day how she could see that way all the time, and she said it was the way she has learned to look at things as she grew older. So it must be her glasses."

The world would be a far better place if all of us could form the good habit of looking at things through Grandma's glasses.

It is obvious that Grandma not only looks through rose-colored glasses, but love-tinted glasses.

As the song of a few years ago so ably expressed it: "What the world needs now is love, sweet love." The world also needs:

A little more kindness and a little less creed;
A little more giving and a little less greed;
A little more smile and a little less frown;
A little less kicking a man when he's down.

A little more "we" and a little less "I";
A little more laugh and a little less cry;
A few more flowers on the pathway of life,
And fewer on the graves at the end of the strife."

Keep on looking through these glasses, and life, for you, will be looking up.

Don't Let Go

Two physicians report that a young man in the army breaks out with hives because he is "allergic to work." Someone should have asked the doctors to keep this quiet. I can foresee an outbreak of this allergy which could reach epidemic proportions.

Already there are thousands of folks who, at the sight of work, must break out in a rash—they seldom break out in a sweat. But we must remember that the Good Book says, "Whatsoever thy hand findeth to do, do it with thy might."

Determination. Persistence. Tenacity. These are attributes so desperately needed in this day.

A man, deep in the depths of despair and discouragement, ready to surrender in the battle of life, came across this poem that sent him back into the battle with new courage and determination to keep on keeping on. Heed these words:

I want to let go, but I won't let go.
There are battles to fight,
By day and night,
For God and the right—
And I'll never let go.

    I want to let go, but I won't let go.
    I'm sick, 'tis true,
    Worried and blue,
    And worn through and through,
    But I won't let go.

I want to let go, but I won't let go.
I will never yield!
What! Lie down on the field
And surrender my shield?
No, I'll never let go!

    I want to let go, but I won't let go.
    May this be my song
    'Mid legions of wrong—
    Oh, God, keep me strong
    That I may never let go!

Live Churches Look beyond Themselves

In the course of my reading, I came across a pointed statement of the definition of live churches as differentiated from dead churches.

You can be the judge of the veracity of each comparison, but at any rate, these assumptions are thought provoking.

Live churches have many noisy children and young people; dead churches are painfully quiet. (Before the service began, a wife reacting to loud sounds around her said to her husband: "Do you hear all that laughing and talking?" "Yes," replied her husband, "and isn't it wonderful?")

Live churches have parking problems; dead churches do not. (This is a good problem to have. Space available in the parking lot usually means space available in the pews.)

Live churches change methods; dead churches do not. ("We've never done it that way before" may not be reason enough to halt every new venture.)

Live churches evangelize; dead churches fossilize. (Reaching out prevents rigor mortis from setting in.)

Live churches move out on faith; dead churches operate totally on sight. (A church that can see no further than its immediate horizon has no vision.)

Live churches are filled with tithers; dead churches are filled with tippers. (Considering the high cost of living, congregations should be reminded that there is no such thing as a progressive "coin-operated" church.)

Live churches support missions enthusiastically and unselfishly with sacrificial giving; dead churches care only for themselves. (In a very real sense, the spiritual vitality of our churches depends upon their response to the mission needs of a lost world.)

Avoid Heart Trouble by Attending Church

Medical research done at Johns Hopkins University says the incidence of fatal heart disease among infrequent churchgoers is twice as high as for men who attend church at least once a week.

The new findings by Dr. George W. Comstock, professor of epidemiology, were reported in the *Journal of the American Medical Association*, but many pastors had long ago assumed that all those who do not attend church at least once a week had a "heart" problem of some kind.

Now the faithful wife has scientific support for seeking to persuade her husband that going to church every Sunday is better for you than fishing or playing golf.

Moreover, there is every reason to believe going to church would counteract HSMS, an ancient virus that poisons the mind and soul. Its victims suffer unusual attacks of slothfulness on all Sunday mornings just before church time.

Those afflicted with Holy Sabbath Morning Sickness become suddenly groggy, habitually grouchy, and shockingly wobbly. It has been said that almost half the membership of our churches "suffer" from this nasty little virus.

Going to church would cure this ailment along with others, such as allergies like pollinosis and hay fever caused, of course, by wild flowers sniffed by those who claim they "worship" better in the outdoors.

In addition to the chronic absentee from church, there is a vast multitude of others—entire families—who seem to regard church as they do a political convention: they send just one delegate.

This overlooks a great truth as shared by Ross Hersey who said, "If I were to make one guess as to what our country needs, it is a return of its people to church."

Still, the establishment of churchgoing as good for one's health is an encouraging and logical step in the right direction.

After all, the church, in its truest sense, has been called "a hospital for sinners."

True Humility

It was reported by John M. Drescher that a five-year-old was speaking to her baby sister while they played in the backyard. She spoke concerning family devotions. "Come on. We are going to have our *demotions*."

This small girl unknowingly hit upon a great truth: "He must increase, but I must decrease."

Many times as believers we need to kneel before our Lord to see once again our own unworthiness and His exceeding grace. Humility is a grace you have already lost when you think you have it. I am told one man wrote a book entitled *Humility and How I Attained It.*

Perhaps you heard of the preacher who said he had a wonderful sermon on humility, and he was just waiting for a large crowd to preach it.

Love has been described as an unselfish grace, and humility is spoken of as an unconscious grace. True humility cannot be counterfeited since it is most prominently seen in the area of lowly service. The humble person is anxious that God receive the glory.

Humility does not come from pious speech. True humility is an unconscious grace which results from a proper estimate of our own unworthiness.

The story has it that a father and son were walking down a city street where a skyscraper was under construction. Looking up they saw men at work on the top story of the building.

"Daddy," said the boy. "What are those little boys doing up there?"

"Those are not little boys; those are grown men, son."

"But why do they look so small?"

"Because they are so high," his father answered.

After a moment's reflection, the boy declared, "Then, when they get to heaven, there won't be anything left of them, will there?"

So it is. The nearer we come to Christ, the less others see of us and the more they see of Christ.

Sleepy Talk

It all started when a local defense agency official asked the pastor of a large city church how many his church could sleep in case of a surprise bomb attack.

"Well," he replied in a burst of honesty, "on Sunday morning we sleep about 200."

Truth is, many a preacher would have to admit that sometimes in the midst of delivering his sermons, it is difficult to catch the eye of his congregation—especially when you consider that so many eyes are closed in sweet repose.

"Not only do they sleep," declared one preacher, "But it's apparent they enjoy it."

Of course, it does not do a whole lot for the preacher's self-confidence in his preaching when the man who has slept during the entire sermon pauses long enough at the door as he leaves to give the parson a firm handshake and say, "Thank you, preacher—that message was just what I needed."

Moreover, there was an actual case reported in which a woman bade farewell to the preacher at the close of the service by saying, "Thanks for the sermon, pastor—I woke up refreshed."

This is a serious new development. For it is a well-known fact that we have depended upon the ladies all these years to keep the men awake in church. After all, the sharpest point during the sermon was often the one at the end of the watchful wife's elbow.

At any rate, both young and older members of most congregations are aware of the problem. In one particular church, coffee is always served after the minister's sermon on Sunday.

One day, in the children's sermon, the minister asked a small boy if he knew why that was done.

The little fellow paused only a few seconds before saying: "I think it's done to wake everybody up before they drive home."

Use It or Lose It!

I am not a camera buff as such. Even in overseas travel, I was not one of those tourists with a camera around his neck who took a picture of everything that moved.

However, it does not require much persuasion on the part of my wife to convince me to pick up a roll of film for use in making pictures of our granddaughter.

Purchasing some film for my camera, I noted on the carton that if I did not use it within a specified time, I could not expect favorable results. It was a matter of use it or lose it!

The same thing is true of a medicinal prescription. If one leaves it too long unused in the medicine chest, chances are it will lose its potency and may even become harmful. It is a matter of using it or losing it.

This is true of the battery in your automobile.

It is true of a muscle in your body, for muscles that go unused tend to grow useless. It is a matter of use or lose.

This is also an inflexible principle of the spiritual life.

Fail to use a talent that you could use in the service of God, and you may suddenly discover that you have lost the talent.

Fail to use the resources that you have in God's service, and you may lose the resources.

So, use what you have for God and your church—your voice in the choir, your ability to teach, your prayers, your gifts—use all for the glory of God.

And you shall find that what you give away—the treasures you lay up in heaven—you keep!

More than a Lick on the Head

Ken Lyle, executive director of the New England Baptist Convention, writes a weekly column for his state paper in which he makes clever use of illustrations from comic strips and cartoons to put over a point.

One "Peanuts" episode pictured Linus and Lucy on the way to school, lunch pails in hand.

She speaks first: "You know, I believe I would have made a good evangelist."

Linus remains thoughtfully silent as his comic strip companion continues to speak: "You remember that boy who sits behind me at school?"

Still no answer from Linus who trudges on toward the schoolhouse.

Not dismayed by his lack of response, Lucy confronts Linus: "I convinced that boy that my religion was better than his religion."

"How did you do that?" inquired Linus.

She replied, "I hit him with my lunch box!"

Several truths are evident.

Like Lucy, every Christian is commanded to be a good witness. Sad to say, many professing Christians never share Christ with anyone.

And others, with good intentions, do bear witness for Christ, but they often use the "hit them over the head" approach to evangelism.

By beating others into submission, they try to convince them that "my religion is better than yours."

In one sense, this method is not sharing the Good News—but the bad news.

To know Christ in an ever-growing relationship is to have the desire to tell others about Him and to live Christ before them.

This does not mean that we are to "hit people over the head"—but we are to touch their hearts for Christ's sake.

Success Begins with Work

Observance of Labor Day should remind us, in the finest and fullest sense, that for the Christian, stewardship of life under God requires that we give our best to the task at hand.

Many have tried over the years, but the fact remains that in any successful endeavor, there is simply no substitute for hard work.

Often you come in contact with someone who works harder to keep from working than he would in actually working.

That could be the reason one astute observer offered this comment: "All that some guys leave behind is seat prints on the sands of time."

Somewhere I came across these wise observations on the contribution that work makes to any lasting success: The Father of success is Work.

The Mother of success is Ambition—especially if it is the right kind of ambition aimed at a worthy purpose and constructive cause.

The eldest Son of success is Common Sense—which is becoming extremely scarce in our day.

Others in the Success Family are: Perseverance, Enthusiasm, and Cooperation. Work cannot be a reality without any of these.

And so, it all comes down to this: if you want to be a part of the Success Family, you must first become acquainted with the "Father" of success, which is work.

Do this and in any worthwhile project, you will be establishing a close relationship with other members of the Success Family, including Cheerfulness, Loyalty, Sincerity, and Harmony.

Strengthening Each Other

Faith in God is a gift that brings strength out of weakness.

And to call on your faith in time of deepest need not only strengthens you, but brings strength to those around you.

Norman Vincent Peale recalled an incident from his ministry of many years ago that supports this truth.

In this particular family there was a little boy eight years old who had a sister age twelve. They lived in Brooklyn, and along with their parents were a part of Peale's congregation.

One night their father died suddenly. Peale went to see them, and the little boy met him in the hall and said, "Pastor, I've got to be strong. I'm the man of the house now."

Peale put his arm around him and said, "Yes, Freddie, you're the man of the house now, and God will help you to be strong."

Then the sister came to the pastor and said, "Daddy is gone—I've got to be strong. Mother is crushed, and Freddie, he's just a kid. I've got to take charge."

"Yes, honey," the pastor replied, "God will help you to carry the load."

Then he went in and sat with the mother. She said, "For the children's sake, I must be strong. I'm both mother and father now. I've got to stand up to it."

"You will do it," the pastor said, "God will enable you to stand."

And Peale said that through the years he watched them—the three of them—abiding in the strength of God and the strength of each other.

In their life's journey, they continued strong with a faith in God that brought strength out of weakness.

Going Hand in Hand

"One family under God" sounds good, but is it really true?

The Bible identifies members of the human race as a family.

The New Testament continues the basic concept of the kinship of those made in God's image.

But even though prophets of the Old Testament declared our need to love one another—we have not always loved our fellowman as we should.

We have cried, "Peace," when there was no peace.

Surely, many would agree that the family of man needs to be filled with a new compassion, touched by a new mercy and lifted by a new love for one another.

As Christians, we must search for a better way to communicate, strive for a sincere way to express love and seek a better understanding.

How can this be done? An old sermon illustration provided the answer. Some years ago, a beautiful little girl living in a rural mountain community strayed away from her home late one afternoon.

It was a bitterly cold winter day—made even more biting by the approach of night.

As news of the missing child circulated through the community, the alarm was sounded and neighbors and friends turned out to look for the lost child.

They covered the lakeside, they combed the woods and marched through the fields. But it was to no avail. They did not find her.

Then, as the darkness of the night deepened, one man suggested that they join hands and move together in their search.

In a short time, the frantic parents were summoned. The child was found, but it was too late. As they stood in a circle and looked down at that frozen lifeless form, someone sobbed, "Oh, God, why didn't we join hands sooner?"

It is a question for all of us. We must join hands and hearts in love and move through life's wilderness to rescue a lost world. And we must do so—before it is too late.

Cornstalks and Confidence

When in my travels I pass through the delightful Georgia town of Washington, I often think of Robert Toombs.

The main street of Washington is named Toombs Avenue in honor of the famous Civil War leader.

In supporting the South's secession before the war began, Toombs is reported to have said, "We can beat those Yankees with cornstalks!"

After the South's defeat and the war had ended, someone chided Toombs for his ill-fated claim. He remained undaunted and calmly replied, "Well, it's true. We could have whipped the Yankees with cornstalks. The only trouble was, they wouldn't fight with cornstalks!"

This is something of a commentary on today's world. As Tony Cartledge reminds us: We are in a spiritual battle with Satan and, like the Yankees, he won't let us choose the weapons!

We are tempted and tested at our most vulnerable points. Where our armor is weakest, and we are most susceptible, Satan's attack is strongest.

In these changing times, we must trust in the Christ who changest not. If we would win the battle, we must follow the leadership of the Supreme Commander who said, "My grace is sufficient for you, for power is perfected in weakness." (2 Corinthians 12:9)

Against the battles of the world, our weapons must often seem no more than cornstalks. But when we take up and put on the whole armor of God, we are "equipped to stand against the wiles of the devil."

And with this armor of the Lord we shall "be able to withstand in the evil day." (Ephesians 6:11, 13)

And the Lord's great strength plus enduring faith and commitment can transform cornstalks into the confidence of ultimate victory.

Someone Watches and Waits

Do you remember the last time you watched a small child learning to swim?

Usually mother launches the youngster while daddy stands a short distance away, arms outstretched, urging the child to come to him.

Everyone shouts encouragement: "Swim! You can do it! Come on! Daddy is waiting!"

And then the child, keeping his eyes on daddy, paddles and kicks with all of his might to reach the promised safety of those outstretched arms.

We never should underestimate the importance of having someone waiting at the finish line—whether we be young or old.

It is a warm, secure feeling to know that someone you love is cheering you on.

As I have said before, all of the machinery of the world would run more smoothly if it were lubricated regularly with the oil of appreciation.

Mothers appreciate a lot of cheering and, while dad might be slow to admit it, he, too, likes a pat on the back.

There are times in life when we feel no one is waiting or watching as we plug away toward the finish line.

But in the larger, finer sense the Christian can be certain that Someone is watching and waiting at the finish line—waiting with arms of love that shall never let us go.

Fact is, it is knowing this that makes swimming in difficult waters easier.

Even when life requires us to swim upstream, there is always the finish line and the One who waits there at the place He has prepared for us.

Will Your Anchor Hold?

I have always found inspiration in the old hymn that goes:

Will the clouds unfold their wings of strife?
When the strong tides lift, and the cables strain,
Will your anchor drift, or firm remain?"

This is an excellent question to ponder in the midst of this stress-filled and perplexing day through which we must pass.

All who are cognizant of the pulls and pressures of these days should do some serious soul searching to make certain that the character of their faith is adequate for every requirement.

We must be able to say, as did the apostle Paul: "In all these things we are more than conquerors through Him that loved us." (Romans 8:37)

As the needs are large, so must our vision and faith be even larger.

Faith starts with small beginnings, a tiny seed planted in our hearts by God. Tiny as it is, God's seed has the potential to grow.

But, as someone has said, before our faith can grow, we need to say "Yes" to all the possibilities God has for us, and to say "No" to our fears.

We must look at the large scene of life through the eyes of faith.

Never let it be said that the chief result of our lack of faith has been that we were content to make small what ought to be large.

We can expand our horizons by cultivating lives that are Christ-centered. In Christ we find the changeless power of the universe.

Our basic faith must be increasingly placed in the Christ Who changest not.

Will your anchor hold? As the chorus of the hymn says:

[In Christ] we have an anchor that keeps the soul
Steadfast and sure while the billows roll.
Fastened to the rock which cannot move,
Grounded firm and deep in the Saviour's love.

This anchor holds!

It Is the Season . . .

As the Christmas carol reminds us, "Tis the season to be jolly," and for many persons the joy is experienced in both giving and receiving gifts.

How did the practice of giving gifts during the holiday season originate?

One researcher claims it was started in Asia Minor during the days of the Holy Roman Empire by the Bishop of Lycia—St. Nicholas.

The bishop had a good friend who was struggling to provide a living for three daughters. Taking pity on his friend, the bishop tossed a purse containing gold coins through his window.

It gave him such a warm, good feeling that he did the same thing the next night.

The word got around, and others began tossing purses through windows of deserving friends. But as time went on, folks began giving other gifts and limited it to the eve that came to be known as Christmas Eve.

Since that time, observing Christmas has become as varied as the people themselves who join in the observance.

One woman, telling her next-door neighbor about Christmas at her house, said: "I was visited by a jolly, bearded fellow with a big bag over his shoulder. It turned out to be my son Josh—home from college with a semester's load of dirty clothes!" So much for Christmas surprises.

In another incident related to the yuletide season, a man who lived in an apartment with valet parking called for his car one morning about two weeks before Christmas and drove off for work.

On the dashboard he noticed a colorful little greeting card which read: "Merry Christmas from all the boys in the garage."

He thought nothing about it until two days before Christmas when he found another card stuck in the same place. It read, "Merry Christmas from all the boys in the garage—Second Notice."

Christmas is the time when many want their past forgotten and their presents remembered.

But true Christmas joy comes in remembering the gift of God's only Son and the gift of salvation through faith in Him.

Living Erroneously

Poet Edgar A. Guest once said, "It takes a heap o' livin' in a house t' make it home."

To go a step further, it could be said from the Christian standpoint that it takes a lot of *right* living to make a life more than just a mere existence.

The following items represent, for most of us, some of the common errors in living:

(1) To attempt to establish your own standards of right and wrong and expect everybody to conform to them.

The natural response to this attitude might be the question from the Scripture, "Who appointed you judge over Israel?"

Our standards will be to little avail in the lives of others unless we have embraced the Lord's standards.

In these perplexing times the only safe time framework within which we may operate is C.S.T.—Christ's Standard Time.

(2) To expect uniformity of opinion.

Not only is this difficult to attain in our day—it is impossible. Achieving uniformity and unanimity is about as easy as changing the law of gravity.

In fact, it is no exaggeration to say that "where two or three Baptists are gathered together, there could be two or three differing opinions."

(3) The third error in living is to look for perfection in others. The age-old problem: some will accept their shortcomings, but not the imperfections of others.

You recall that the man who said to a pastor, "When I find the perfect church, I will join it," was told, "If you ever find the perfect church, then don't join it, for when you join, it will no longer be perfect."

One way to correct this error in living is to remember the Scripture, which teaches that we are to be judged as we judge others, and we are to be forgiven to the same degree that we forgive others.

Keep these truths in your heart, and your life will be looking up.

Largest Living Thing on Earth?

This is not a riddle. It is a serious question: What is the largest living thing on earth? I have seen the giant Sequoia California redwood trees that rise more than 300 feet into the air. But even this tree does not qualify as "the largest living thing on earth."

As a small boy, I once saw a large whale on display—and it seemed to be huge at the time. But as I grew older and a bit larger, I realized that even this big creature could not have been the largest of God's living creations.

However, scientists at the University of Toronto in Ontario made a startling discovery of what they claimed to be the largest living thing on earth: a fungus in the Upper Peninsula of Michigan.

Called an Armillaria Bulbosa, this giant mold is the size of twenty football fields or thirty acres, weighs forty tons and is still growing! But now, scientists in southwestern Washington report a fungus that is forty times bigger. The Armillaria Ostoyae covers 1,500 acres or two-and-a-half square miles.

Whatever else this does, it certainly gives new meaning to the old saying, "as big as all outdoors." And although this may be an accurate commentary on our times, it is sad to know that "the largest living thing on earth" is a fungus.

It does seem to me that there was a time when we, the people, were larger of heart than we are now. Surely, there are many who can remember in other times when many hearts appeared to be bigger than the lowly fungus.

And yet, I prefer to look on the brighter side and join with all those who believe that love continues to be the largest living thing on earth.

Love that endures, love that never fails, is bigger than life itself. Love, of course, is bigger and stronger than fellowship. But fellowship as a living thing is a big improvement over a major group of parasitic lower plants called a "fungus."

Blessing in the Fog

The biography of English poet William Cowper reveals that in 1754 he began to show signs of mental disorder. Subject to fits of depression, he would lose his reason temporarily which resulted in an attempt to commit suicide in 1763. One day, as he was staggering in the depths of despondency, he ordered a carriage and told the driver to rush him to the London Bridge.

While en route, a dense fog blanketed the city and made it impossible for the driver to see the road and find the way to Cowper's desired destination. After wandering about in an aimless pattern for two hours, the driver had to admit he was lost and had no idea where they were.

Cowper asked the driver if he thought he could find the way back to his home. The driver thought he could, and when another hour had passed, Cowper was safely delivered to his door.

When Cowper asked what the fare was, the driver argued that he should not take anything since he had not been able to take his passenger to his destination. But Cowper insisted on paying him, declaring, "Never mind that, you have saved my life! I was on my way to throw myself off the London Bridge!"

The poet then went into his house and, in an inspired moment, wrote:

God moves in a mysterious way
His wonders to perform;
He plants his footsteps in the sea
And rides upon the storm.

It is often true that the light of a new day, the light of a new life, the light of new strength waits on the other side of the fog.

"For now we see through a glass, darkly; but then, face to face; now I know in part, but then shall I know even as also I am known." (1 Corinthians 13:12)

And so it is that we can join in singing the hymn: "The darkness deepens; Lord, with me abide. . . . "

For as Paul said: "And we know that all things work together for good to them that love God, to them who are the called according to his purpose." (Romans 8:28)

Family: Fuss, Feud, Fun, or Faith?

Christian Home Week underlines the importance of holding the home together with God and each other in this frenzied day.

Someone has accurately described the American home as "a domestic cloverleaf on which we pass one another on the way to other feverish pursuits." All of which brings us to this pertinent point of light: "Kindness goes a long way, when a lot of times it ought to stay at home."

Fact is, in the understanding, loving, Christian relationship, kindness should begin and continue in the home.

A lawyer and a Christian psychologist were making small talk at a dinner meeting.

"You and your wife get along very well," said the lawyer. "Do you ever have differences of opinion?"

"Definitely," said the psychologist, "very often. But we get over them quickly."

"How do you do that?" asked the lawyer.

"Simple," said the psychologist. "I never tell her about them."

This observation supports the opinion of some that "A good marriage is like a casserole. Only those responsible for it really know what goes into it."

But among the essentials for a successful home, we would have to list a sense of humor. It is said that in a certain small town the people were jubilant. The meanest man in town married the gossipiest woman, and now, it was said, they won't spoil two households.

Then, there was the husband who said, "There are many women who enjoy doing housework." His wife said, "Great! Let's hire one!"

But more important to the success of the Christian home is the spiritual family heritage that some have been privileged to enjoy.

List all who contributed to your acceptance of Jesus as Lord of your life: Christian parents, Sunday School teachers, pastors, and Christian friends who made an indelible impression on your life. Their marks are still upon you and emerge as forces for good in your home now and always.

And because of this heritage, family fuss can be turned into fun and faith.

Truth

Josh Billings, old-time humorist and punster, once said: "As scarce as truth is, the supply has always been in excess of the demand."

Admittedly, it could be said that in these times there are a good many persons who deal, but not too many who deal in the truth.

"Sedentary work," said the college lecturer, "tends to lessen the endurance."

"In other words," chimed in the smart student, "the more one sits, the less one can stand."

"Exactly," replied the lecturer, "and if one lies a great deal, one's standing is lost completely."

There is a significant application here. One falls with falsehood, but stands on the truth.

In the eighth chapter of the Gospel of John, verses 31 and 32 read: "Jesus therefore was saying to those Jews who had believed in him, 'If you abide in my word, then you are truly disciples of mine; and you shall know the truth, and the truth shall make you free.' "

Jesus is saying here that it is essential that we recognize and remain loyal to the truth.

Josh Billings may have been right. Most of us want truth applied to others instead of to ourselves.

But you and I know what truth is. Truth is that sense of rightness at the very heart of life that needs no proof, no defense and no verification.

Truth does not have to be propped up. Truth stands on its own.

You can build on truth. But without truth, the structure of life falls apart.

Stand with the truth, and you can move through life in good standing.

Living in the Victory of the Empty Tomb

Good Friday and Easter Sunday flood the mind with observations concerning this glad day.

One day during the French Revolution, a man remarked to Tallyrand, who at the time was bishop of Autun: "The Christian religion—what is it? It would be easy to start a religion like that."

"Oh, yes," replied Tallyrand. "One would only have to be crucified and rise again on the third day."

This is well said. It is the appropriate reply to those who would stoop to take anything away from the crucifixion and resurrection of our Lord.

During the lifetime of the late President Calvin Coolidge, a campaign was begun to discredit George Washington and rob him of the renown and affection he had won as the "Father of his Country."

A friend asked Mr. Coolidge, "What is your opinion of the 'Discredit Washington' movement?"

The president lifted his eyes to look for a moment at the Washington Monument, towering 555 feet into the air. And then, with his usual candor and straightforwardness, he replied, "I see the monument is still there."

When so-called doubters scoff at the Resurrection story with all of its wonderful implications, Faith is able to point them to a spot in the land of Faith's beginning and say, "I see the empty tomb is still there!"

As the popular hymn expresses it so well, "Because he lives, I can face tomorrow."

And that is important—to be able to face tomorrow.

But it is no less important to be able to face today with all of its problems and perplexities.

The good news is that the empty tomb is still there. And because He lives, we can face today and tomorrow with victorious faith.

Are You Listening?

With any degree of discernment, it should be noted that listening is rapidly becoming a lost art.

There are so many voices clamoring for attention in this frantic day—some of which are not worthy of one's full concentration—that it is easy to make the mistake of tuning out everything.

Failing to listen can be detrimental to learning and assimilating knowledge, which is essential to both mental and spiritual development.

There comes to mind a man of unusual intelligence who is "up on everything" and conversant on any subject. True, he is well read, but the secret of his mental and spiritual alertness is that he listens.

If anyone is conversing in his presence, he gives his undivided attention—fixing both eyes and ears on the person who is speaking.

This is not true of those who welcome distractions—even when they are being addressed eyeball to eyeball.

A contributing factor in all of this is that many of us are more concerned with formulating our answer than in listening to what is being discussed.

A lady in Edinburgh, Scotland, was totally opposed to street-corner evangelism. One Sunday evening she was waiting for a streetcar at a location frequently used by street evangelists.

The message had just ended when, to her horror, she saw that the evangelist was coming in her direction. She gathered her strength and had her answer ready.

So when the street preacher approached her and said, "Excuse me, madam, but does the number six car go to Marchmont?" she snapped back, "That's a matter between me and my God!"

She answered a question that wasn't asked. She hadn't heard the man because she was, as they say, "listening with her answer running."

Are you listening? It is important that we hear the questions of others. But it is even more important that we hear the voice of God speaking to us.

And for all of us, the most significant form of communication by prayer is the simple practice of listening to God.

How Do You Walk the Walk?

As we journey through life, it is a well-known fact that even for the dedicated Christian, it is so much easier to "talk the talk" than it is to "walk the walk."

And yet, our steps speak more loudly than our words.

It would be a good idea for each of us to check up on ourselves from time to time, and find out if we are actually being of service to our fellowman as we walk along the road of life.

How did I do today?

Is anybody happier
Because you passed this way?
Will anyone remember
That you spoke to him today?

When this day is almost over
And its toiling time is through;
Will there be anyone to utter
A friendly word of you?

Can you say tonight in passing,
With the day that slipped so fast,
That you helped a single person
Of the many that you passed?

Is a single heart rejoicing
Over what you did or said?
Does one whose hopes are fading
Now with courage look ahead?

Did you waste the day or lose it?
Was it well or poorly spent?
Did you leave a trail of kindness
Or a scar of discontent?

What kind of trail are you leaving?

Let it be a trail of lovingkindness, and you will be walking in the finest way. In fact, in word and deed, you will be walking God's highway of life. And this is looking up.

Troubled Breathing

On the way to a speaking engagement, I was driving south on Interstate 75.

It was mid-morning, coffee break time, and I turned off at an exit that led to a fast-food stop where I remembered that the coffee was good and the warm cinnamon rolls even better.

When you travel thousands of miles a year within the state, the faces of restaurant employees become familiar.

I smiled and spoke to an elderly woman, past retirement age, who was working at the hard task of mopping floors and clearing tables. She was too old to work, but too poor to quit.

I remembered her from other visits, and somehow she knew this. Maybe she thought she saw a friendly face in the crowd.

At any rate, she began to talk: "I'm having trouble breathing this morning," she said. "I hope it's not fluid building up around my heart again."

"I join you in that hope," I said, "and I'll be praying for you."

Returning to my car, I drove back onto the highway and resumed my journey. But the incident with the woman at the restaurant would not leave my mind.

She represents the vast army of little-known and often forgotten people of the world who want to share their deepest concerns with someone.

They are the last, the least, and, frequently, the lost who, in a very real sense, feel a kind of suffocation sweeping over them.

As the pain of life closes in, they have many breathless moments.

They need to know that a strong faith in the Lord of life can be—under any circumstances—like a breath of fresh air.

And those of us who call ourselves Christians must be ready and willing to listen with sympathetic ears to the sad song of humanity while extending the hand of concern and compassion.

Our Lord said it: "Verily I say unto you, inasmuch as you have done it unto one of the least of these my brethren, you have done it unto me." (Matthew 25:40)

Bold Enough to Fail

Robert Browning once said: "Ah, but a man's reach should exceed his grasp, or what's a heaven for?" In this famous quotation, Browning spoke of the necessity of setting goals related to our potential. He was saying in the word of today, one is to stretch himself to his full potential.

It is almost a universal characteristic when people talk about their cherished goals, there is a faraway look in their eyes indicative of their hopes for something beyond or ahead of them. Yet, for some, the envisioning of lofty goals is fraught with fear. There are many examples of this.

Maslow declared, "We fear our highest possibilities. We are generally afraid to become that which we glimpse in our loftiest moments, under the most perfect conditions, under the conditions of greatest courage."

We enjoy the possibilities that we see in ourselves in such peak moments. And yet, there are those who seem to shiver in weakness and fear as they look toward these very same possibilities.

Perhaps the reason for this fear is the possibility of failure. Rather than to aspire toward that greatest potential and risk failure, many suppress the desire to achieve and rob themselves of their greatest potential for growth.

I remember preparing a sermon entitled "Bold Enough to Fail." The premise of the message was that if we hold off and do not seek to reach a goal because we fear we may not reach that goal, then we will never really attempt anything.

Most people who have achieved great things have also failed in many things before they crossed the victory line. One man said: "If I did not fear failure, I could do almost anything!" One hurdle that hinders many is fear of failure.

You see, it isn't the economy, it isn't the weather, it isn't the boss, it isn't the laws of supply and demand that holds us back. The thing that holds us back from great progress is fear of failure. And only by the strength of Christ can we overcome our own fears. In Christ, we can become bold enough to extend ourselves and seek achievement. In Christ, we can reach up to greater goals.

With Christ and his strength, we can be bold enough to fail. And if we are bold enough to fail, bold enough to try and bold enough to reach for loftier goals, then in the strength of Christ we can do almost anything.

So, let us move forward in faith. Let us be bold enough to fail and in so doing, bold enough to achieve.

Planting a Church Garden

In the spring of the year, the thoughts of many turn toward the planting of their spring gardens. We would do well to concentrate on the planting of another kind of garden—a garden that could result in church growth.

It seems that one Sunday at the close of the morning worship service, the ushers passed out slips of paper to everyone. The paper was brightly decorated with colored pictures of squash, turnips, and lettuce. At the bottom of the page there were suggestions as to how we might "plant" a Church Garden for future growth. The garden should contain:

Three rows of squash:
    (1) Squash indifference.
    (2) Squash destructive criticism.
    (3) Squash gossip.
Four rows of turnips:
    (1) Turn up for all meetings.
    (2) Turn up with a visitor.
    (3) Turn up with your Bible.
    (4) Turn up with a smile.
Five rows of lettuce:
    (1) Let us welcome strangers—with joy and enthusiasm.
    (2) Let us give liberally. "Upon the first day of the week let everyone of you lay by him in store, as God has prospered him." (1 Corinthians 16:2) "So let him give; not grudgingly, or of necessity: for God loveth a cheerful giver." (2 Corinthians 9:7)
    (3) Let us be faithful to duty. "Be thou faithful unto death, and I will give thee a crown of life." (Revelation 2:10)
    (4) Let us truly worship God. "And Jesus answered . . . you shall worship the Lord your God, and Him only shall you serve." (Luke 4:8)
    (5) Let us love one another. "Beloved, let us love one another: for love is of God; and everyone that loveth is born of God, and knoweth God." (1 John 4:7)

Plant your church garden in this way, and under these conditions, and you will be planting for future growth.

Long Distance Love

Long-distance love is so much easier to manage than loving those close at hand.

There is much proof of this. For example, it is so much easier to excite a congregation with the possibility of reaching out in love to a foreign mission field than it is to reach out in love and concern to a lost person living in the same neighborhood.

As one fellow said, "That's the way I like my distant relatives—at a distance."

As further illustration, there was once a professor of child psychology who, although he had no children of his own, was a self-pronounced expert on rearing children.

He would admonish, "Remember, you must always love your children."

On a hot summer afternoon, the professor had just completed work on a concrete driveway. Weary from the strenuous labor, he put down his trowel, wiped sweat from his head, and started into the house.

From the corner of his eye, he spotted a small boy placing his foot in the freshly poured concrete.

Rushing out, he grabbed the child, and was about to spank him when a neighbor said, "Professor, remember you must love the child!"

To which the professor yelled back, "I do love him in the abstract, but not in the concrete!"

Prevalent as it is, long-distance love does not meet God's requirements. "For he that loveth not his brother whom he hath seen, how can he love God whom he hath not seen?" (1 John 4:20)

The Right Kind of Exercise

No doubt you have noticed that almost everybody is on some kind of exercise kick.

Joggers can be seen running along both city and country roads morning, noon, and night.

And in every group conversation someone mentions his or her method of staying in shape.

For several years I have practiced the self-discipline of working out in my basement on a dual-action exercycle every night that I am in town. (My granddaughter, being very observant, had perhaps the wisest comment as she watched me exercise: "It's not a very good bicycle—it doesn't go anywhere.")

But it would be wise to consider what could be a more valuable exercise for all concerned. The following exercises are good for both body and soul.

More of us need to exercise a constant search for *balance* in this strange and perplexing time.

Balance is becoming extremely scarce. Don't run away from reason. Strive for balance.

Why not exercise *restraint*? We need to restrain some of our rhetoric. Before we speak, let us ask ourselves the questions, Is it positive? Is it productive? Above all, is it Christian?

The condition of life around us could be improved by the exercise of restraint.

Let us all resolve to exercise more *patience* with our fellowman. It is apparent that too many among us get most of their exercise from "jumping at conclusions" and "flying off the handle."

Moreover, many of our problems could be solved if we all made an honest effort to exercise more *love and understanding* toward our fellowman.

This is the right kind of exercise that could prolong life and is certain to add to the joy of life.

Secret of Strength

February, as the month in which he was born, serves as a reminder of some of the unusual attributes of Abraham Lincoln, the sixteenth president of the United States.

He had insight and the ability to communicate his convictions so clearly and with such force that millions of his countrymen could understand them and make them their own.

Another valuable asset which set Lincoln apart from so many others was his wonderful sense of humor and his ability to laugh at himself.

After his election, an old friend came up to Lincoln and said, "Tell me, Abe, how does it feel to be president of the United States?"

"Well," Lincoln responded in his typical drawl, "You have heard about the fellow who was tarred and feathered, and was ridden out of town on a rail.

"Some man standing in the crowd, watching the procession as it passed, asked the poor fellow how he liked it.

" 'Well,' he answered, 'I need to say this. If it weren't for the honor of the thing, I would just as soon walk.' "

Lincoln used humor as well as any modern-day comedian, politician, or combination of the two. In one of his many political debates, his opponent repeatedly referred to him as two-faced.

When it was Lincoln's turn to speak, he neutralized his critic's tirade with his first sentence: "Ladies and gentlemen, I ask you, if I were two-faced, would I be wearing this one?"

What is more important is that Lincoln had a spiritual depth and a faith of his own.

It has been said of Lincoln that he was one of the few presidents that put living the Bible above that of talking it.

And, as a result, he was never alone. He had the counsel of God, which outweighed all of the difficulties that came his way.

In Need of Communication

John Naisbitt, in his best-selling book *Megatrends*, underlines the necessity for good communication.

He says we no longer live in an agricultural or industrial society, but instead we are in the age of communication. The author even goes on to say that the future will belong to those who can communicate.

Saying what we mean—and meaning what we say—are important principles of communication.

Often when we think we are saying one thing we are actually communicating something quite different to the listener or reader.

This difficulty is supported by the notice that appeared in a church bulletin: "Tuesday afternoon there will be meetings in the north and south ends of the church. Children will be baptized at both ends."

Daily newspapers are also guilty of frequently failing to communicate the intended thought. Note these newspaper advertisements: "On sale in bargain basement: Shirts for men with minor flaws" and "Shoes for women with slight imperfections."

Such ambiguous wording is something like the memorandum making the rounds in an office: "I know that you believe you understand what you think I said, but I am not sure that you realize that what you heard is not what I meant!"

Let us work hard at communication. Misinformation and misunderstanding are formidable foes of the good, orderly life.

To say what we mean and to mean what we say—and to be understood—are goals worthy of our best efforts.

Self above Service

A well-known civic club has as its altruistic motto "Service above Self." However, there are countless other persons who seem to live by the motto "Self above Service."

Research psychologists, in reexamining the tenets of selfism, state: "New research reveals that the most common error in people's self image is not low self-esteem, but a self-serving bias; not the inferiority complex but the superiority complex."

These research results provide a fresh reaffirmation of the old Christian wisdom concerning the pervasiveness of pride.

As the apostle Paul said, "For I say, through the grace given unto me, to every man that is among you, not to think of himself more highly than he ought to think. . . . " (Romans 12:3)

Be that as it may, studies indicate that most people rate themselves better than average on almost any scale. This no doubt explains why one good churchman objected to singing the words from the old hymn that said "for such a worthless worm as I" and instead changed the words to the more complimentary note: "for such a worthful worm as I."

Still, the question persists, "Can we all be above average?"

Apparently, many think so. Research shows that most business people see themselves as more ethical than "the average business person." And it naturally follows that most Americans perceive themselves as more intelligent than the average person.

One thing is certain. Research supports the fact that in most instances we do love ourselves very much.

Too often it is a case of love at first sight, and it is an affection for self that grows with each passing year. That is the natural orientation for many.

But the challenge lies in looking away from self toward others and in loving our neighbor.

The Master offered to all of us the perfect workable solution in the commandment "love your neighbor as yourself." (Matthew 22:39)

Don't Throw Cold Water on Someone's Warm Faith

Have you ever considered how important it is that we encourage and affirm one in the faith rather than making the mistake of putting down another's testimony with the cold water of ridicule?

Parents have been known to do this to children, children to parents, and both husbands and wives providing this disservice to each other—all with disastrous results.

Of all times in history, this is a day when we should encourage each other in the faith, lifting up instead of bringing down. We need to follow these words from Scripture: "And he set the priests in their offices and encouraged them in the service of the house of the Lord." (2 Chron 35:2)

These words apply to both ministers and laypersons alike.

There is a sad incident from the life of writer and humorist Mark Twain that speaks so graphically to the fault of putting down rather than building up another's faith. When Twain married Olivia Langdon, she was a very religious and optimistic person, with her faith resting firmly on God. But Twain had no faith, scoffing at her beliefs and making light of her devotions.

Soon Olivia's faith began to diminish. There was a noticeable decline in her prayer life. What had been a warm fire of faith turned to cold ashes of doubt. She did not seem to care anymore. Eventually, she forsook her faith altogether. A deep sorrow covered Olivia's life. Twain loved her and had never intended to hurt her—but he discovered that he had broken her spirit.

"Livy," he said, "if it comforts you to lean on your faith, do so." But it was too late. Sadly, she replied, "I cannot. I do not have any faith left."

This haunted Twain as long as he lived, but the harm was done—the thoughtless act could not be changed.

Let us be certain that we guard against tearing down anyone's faith. Here is a better way for each of us: "And now, brethren, I commend you to God, and to the Word of His grace, which is able to build you up." (Acts 20:32)

All Work Is Important

The most prevalent virus that has hindered many worthwhile projects and halted progress in our time is the virus of "laziness."

It may be couched in unusual terminology, but the fact remains: it is still laziness.

Physicians are often inclined to describe ailments in technical terms, and at times this is helpful.

There was the patient who told his physician: "Doc, I want a thorough examination, and when you are finished, I don't want you to give me a fancy Latin word for what ails me. Give it to me straight in plain English."

When the doctor had completed the examination, he reported: "There is nothing wrong with you; you're just lazy."

The patient then changed his instructions: "Would you please give me the Latin word for that? My wife will ask me what you said."

But nevertheless, laziness is still laziness, and work is work. All work is important. A professor once said; "If all the garbage men and all the preachers quit at the same time, which would you miss first?"

The point is not to downgrade preachers but to focus on the importance of all work. Honest work demands our best, and we should give our best.

A small boy on his first day in kindergarten looked at everything—the low tables and chairs, little cupboards, small coat hangers, low sink and said to the teacher: "I don't like it here. There's nothing to grow up to."

Truth is, we do need to extend ourselves. Computers are replacing many persons who work with their minds, but nothing can ever replace the finest physical instrument of all—the human hand.

This is especially true when that hand is a willing, working hand extended in love and concern for the work of God and the good of man.

Living Up to Mother's Love

Henry Ward Beecher once said that "the mother's heart is the child's best schoolroom."

Certainly this would be true of the good and faithful mother who is deserving of all honor.

It is rather easy to distinguish an effective mother from an ineffective one. Someone told of watching an ineffective mother of a five-year-old who was loose and running wild in a grocery store.

He had already toppled two displays of canned goods and one stack of bakery products before his mother called out feebly, "Now, Sonny, don't do that."

A few more minutes passed, and in that brief span of time saltine crackers and canned beans littered the floor as the boy raced through the store.

When he reached the area near the checkout counters, he began his attack on the magazine rack. His mother did manage to utter a weak, "Please be careful." But those witnessing this disaster in the making were more concerned for the safety of the store.

Sticking his toes into the wire mesh of the magazine rack, the little fellow began to climb to the top—and then it happened: he crashed to the floor, and magazines sailed in all directions. But in all of this, there had been no real correction or discipline of the child.

Contrast this with an effective mother I once saw who wisely handled a difficult situation. Even with a guest in the home, the boy was "acting up" in the worst possible way.

The mother remained calm but firm. And then, with great love for the cantankerous boy, she turned to the visitor and said, "I want to apologize for John. Right now, he is acting in a terrible way. But he really is a very fine boy—and I wanted you to know that."

The boy heard her words and immediately changed his conduct. He was a good boy, and through the years as he grew to manhood he proved it by living up to his mother's love.

Don't Stop—Keep Playing!

There are many stories connected with the concert pianist Ignacy Paderewski that serve to illustrate great truths.

One time, a doting mother, desiring to encourage her son's progress on the piano, bought tickets for a Paderewski performance.

Locating their seats near the front of the concert hall, the mother discovered a friend and began to visit with her. The boy, unobserved, got up and slipped away.

When eight o'clock arrived, the mother missed her small son, but as the spotlights came on, she was astonished to see her son on stage, at the piano, busily picking out his own version of "Twinkle, Twinkle, Little Star."

A wave of nervous laughter passed through the audience as Paderewski appeared on stage and swiftly moved to the keyboard.

The audience speculated on what the master musician would do under these unusual circumstances. Smiling, Paderewski leaned over and whispered to the boy, "Don't quit—keep playing."

The old master then reached down with his left hand and began filling in a bass part. In a moment, his right arm reached around the other side, encircling the boy, to add another new dimension to the impromptu duet.

Together, the old master and the young boy held the crowd spellbound.

There is an obvious truth here for each of us. In this frantic day, there is much discord all about us.

But in the midst of it all, the Master, Jesus Christ, whispers in our ear, "Don't quit—keep playing!"

And as we continue to give our best, the Lord joins us in what we're trying to do, blesses our efforts, and turns discord into beautiful music.

Take Time to Smell the Roses

An old-timer, who had gained some following as a country-store, crossroads philosopher, once said, "It just don't pay to be in too much of a hurry—you just pass up more than you catch up with." He has a point there—a good point.

As you sit and watch the world go by with its hectic craving for pleasure, power, prestige, and self-gratification, you could wish someone would turn the spotlight on simpler joys of life:

The joy of walking down a country road or along a running stream.

The joy of hard work with the realization that achievement is its own reward.

The joy of hearing the laughter of children at play, a bird's song, and a church bell that calls people to prayer.

Then, too, there is the joy of being inspired by an outstanding church choir, hearing scripture read well and feeling strength of corporate worship.

There is the beauty of a flower garden, where wisdom demands that one take the time to smell the roses.

And what of the beauty of a sunset or the welcome sight of a sunrise.

Then, there is the beautiful sight of the first star at night and the first glimpse of a full moon.

Or the cooling, refreshing feel of rain after a hot day. And the too-seldom-seen rainbow.

All of which reminds us of precious promises of our Lord who came that our joy might be full.

And best of all, He promised never to leave us or forsake us.

Fear and Faith

"These are the times that try men's souls."

And because these are trying times in every sense of the word, this could be described as the age of fear.

Some are filled with regrets over what happened yesterday, shaken with nervous anticipation of what today may bring, and hopelessly afraid of tomorrow.

The argument goes like this: so many things can happen in one's life—failure, loneliness, illness, accident, and death.

All are valid fears, in the minds of many, and fear is such a dangerous thing. It can ruin sleep, turn even good food into "unappetizing lumps of sawdust," destroy friendship, diminish love, and make an agony of life.

Sooner or later the question comes to most of us: "Why am I afraid?" Truth is, as Christians we are never alone. God lives. God cares. The Lord is with us—even now.

So the question is, why fear tomorrow when God is with you today?

It is very likely in the daily lives of most of us that worry takes place when we take upon ourselves responsibilities and burdens God never intended us to have.

The old spiritual has the right idea: "I'm gonna lay down my burden, down by the riverside," and then goes on to say, "Ain't gonna study war no more."

Good advice: bring your burdens to the Lord and leave them there, and "as much as lieth in you, live peaceably with all men."

As for fear, live by these words: fear no men. Leave them to God for the settling of all final accounts.

And as you move forward in victory, let this be your only fear: that you may be something less to your Lord than he intended you to be.

Who Sets Your Standards?

There are many ways by which a person's life may be measured.

By what is said,
What is read,
What is prayed,
What is done.

Furthermore, I have always surmised that another important measurement is who and what a person listens to.

You can often see before your very eyes the decline and fall of a person who listens to the wrong people saying the wrong things.

This is a significant question: Who sets your standards?

This old story speaks to the point. In a certain little village a man always stopped by a clock shop to set his watch every morning.

One day the clock shop owner stepped outside and asked this man, "Why do you stop here every morning and set your watch?"

The man replied, "You see, I work at the big factory down the street, and I am in charge of blowing the noon whistle every day. So, to be certain of my accuracy, I stop here every morning to make sure I have the right time."

A strange expression covered the shop owner's face. "That's odd," he said, "I set my clock every day at noon when you blow the whistle."

The application is obvious. Who sets your standards? Are you trying to go through life setting your standards by your own standards?

What are your measurements? Do you operate on your time or on G.S.T.—God's Standard Time?

Our Lord is the only infallible guide—the only compass by which we can chart our course, assured that at journey's end the vessel of life, frail and faulty though it may be, shall reach the distant shore.

A Good Father Is God's Gift

I was speaking in a Georgia church not long ago, and when the service ended a man came up and said, "I remember your dad. He was my Sunday School teacher."

This meant much to me—far more than if the man had said, "I know you." In fact, the conversation kindled warm memories and appreciation for a good father.

By any measurement, a good father is a gift of God's love and a needed gift from God, the Heavenly Father.

When Jesus came to use a term picturing God, He seized upon the term Father. The phrase "our Heavenly Father" became a warm, meaningful description for God. It conveys so much. And when, in these days, we substitute "Parent," I think we lose something in terms of endearment.

When the *Milwaukee Sentinel* reported on a contest in which children were to write letters on the subject "My Pop's Tops," one child wrote in a loving way: "I have such a great time with my father that I wish I had known him sooner."

Dale Murphy, star major-league outfielder, when asked what contribution his father made to his life, replied, "The great thing my dad provided me was himself."

That's a worthy contribution. As actor Bill Cosby said, in commenting on his responsibility as a father, "I am committed to not giving up."

Too often fathers are prone to quit, minimizing their role in the religious training of the children—leaving it all to the mother.

But in addition to himself, there is one thing more a good father gives to his children: a sense of Christian hope.

Few things are more vital to give children than a deep hope in the face of discouragement—the hope that springs eternal from our Christian faith.

Hope is what a good father must give his children today. The hope that God can and does have the power to transform life. Hope that God can bring good out of evil, turn wrong into right, and make the best of the worst.

The Urgency of Witness

He was an old man, past eighty, full of years and wisdom.

Seeing me through the open door to the pastor's study, he came in to share the few minutes that remained before I was to enter the pulpit for the revival service.

I listened to his moving testimony of what Jesus Christ had brought into his life: love, strength, courage, joy, salvation.

We were so caught up in the conversation that the time got away. After all, who wants to pause to look at a watch when one speaks of things eternal?

The sound of the organ prelude signaled approach of the appointed time for the meeting to begin. But there was something else he wanted to say—something he had to say.

"When it comes to witnessing for my Lord," he said, "I have this strong feeling: as a Christian, I don't have the right to withhold from any person my knowledge of the saving power of Jesus Christ. I must share my faith," he declared.

And then, I thought I saw a tear form in his eyes as he said, "It might be my last time to witness, and it could be the last opportunity someone has to hear that word of witness."

I joined the choir in the hallway. We marched in, and the service began.

The conversation with this great old Christian had been a blessing. It may have improved my preaching.

It had reminded me that I, also, "do not have the right to withhold my Christian witness from any person."

Pastor Wrestles "Masked Saint" at Evening Service

The pastor of a church in Oak Ridge, Tennessee, recently wrestled the "Masked Saint" at a special Sunday night service featuring barbecue, preaching, and the wrestling match.

Wrestling?

Now I know what is meant by going to any extreme to increase Sunday night worship attendance.

Even though he was billed as the "Powerhouse Parson," it should be noted that he is not the first preacher who has thrown his weight around.

But there is a distinct difference in that the chest beating and muscle flexing connected with this episode were not restricted to the church conference and business meeting.

And who knows? His professional skill as a wrestler might help him—even in this hectic day—to get a stranglehold on some of his church problems.

However, there could be some question as to the Fall of Man doctrinal and theological soundness of the wrestling match rules which, I understand, declare that "The winner shall be the one who gets the best of two out of three falls."

On the positive side, the event attracted a record crowd of 1,000 persons—half of whom were youth—and the church gained 300 prospects, which accomplished the purpose of bringing people under the influence of the gospel.

And it is certain that those in attendance were reminded that "We wrestle not against flesh and blood, but against principalities, against powers, against the rulers of the darkness of the world, against spiritual wickedness in high places. Wherefore take unto you the whole armor of God, that you may be able to withstand in the evil day." (Eph 6:12-13)

Falling Out Is Dangerous

I read somewhere recently that meteorologists admit that the last accurate weather forecast was when God told Noah it was going to rain.

However, as most pastors will readily declare, it doesn't actually have to rain to reduce church attendance—a threat of rain will cut down on the size of the congregation.

This familiar scene is enacted in so many households across our land.

It is Sunday morning—the day of worship. But at the breaking of the first light, someone rushes to the window, peers out, and shouts, "It looks like rain!"

Others rush to the window to confirm the news. "Yes, that's right. It's clouding up; it's going to rain."

A family conference is hastily called, and they all agree that since the weather is so bad, they can't go to church, so they will go elsewhere.

Since the first rainy Sunday ever recorded, many pastors must have wondered why the weather around the church is so much worse than the weather anywhere else.

And on Sunday night it is a well-known fact that the night air around the church is nothing short of dangerous!

Even long before we heard of nuclear fallout, millions would shudder at the thought of being caught out in the night air surrounding the church.

Admittedly, fallout is dangerous. But falling out and away from the habit of church attendance is also destructive to the spiritual life.

It would be well to heed the scriptural warning from Hebrews 10:25: "not forsaking the assembling of ourselves together as the manner of some is."

Happy Medium

It is not easy in this unusual time to keep the right perspective.

Maintaining one's balance while something or someone continues to rock the boat of life is a daily challenge.

But I do recall the incident involving a group of neighborhood children who apparently came up with the answer.

The children got together and built a little clubhouse in the backyard high up in the oak tree with a ladder nailed on the side of the tree trunk for climbing purposes.

When the work was completed, they sat down, weary but pleased at the results of their cooperative labor.

Somebody said, "Well, if we are going to have a club, we will have to organize and have some club rules."

Another suggested, "Let's have three rules." And so they wrote down the following rules:

Rule number one: Nobody act big.
Rule number two: Nobody act little.
Rule number three: Everybody act medium.

Out of the mouths and minds of these children, there came wisdom. For you know, the most difficult feat in all the world is to act medium.

Judging from the actions of so many of us, the easiest thing in the world to do is to act big or to act little.

The hardest thing to do is to be what you are—to be honest—without pretense—as your true self, warts and all.

Solomon wrote, "Let another praise you, and not your own mouth."

That can be a dangerous time—a time when one begins to believe his own praise. The next step that follows is when we forsake the role of servant and assume the role of commanding officer.

That also is the time when we ignore the needs of others and think first and foremost of our own needs.

It is then that it becomes an acid test for acting medium.

But one thing is certain: if in the midst of today's troubled world, we can manage to act medium, it will be for all of us a happy medium.

Pushing or Riding?

It was early on a Sunday morning, and I was traveling to fill a preaching assignment in one of our Georgia churches.

I stopped at a service station and after filling up at the self-service pump, I was all set to take to the highway again.

Buckling my safety belt, I was reaching for the ignition key when I noticed a lone black man, struggling to push his stalled car back onto the road.

I got out to help, joining him at the back bumper, with the word, "Brother, this is a big job for one man—maybe I can help."

Smiling with appreciation, he put his shoulder to the task and we pushed. Then, to my surprise, I looked up to see through the rear window of his car that he had three passengers—all good-sized children—and all able-bodied and capable of pushing most any size automobile.

My friend in need at the rear bumper had followed my eyes, read my mind, and answered my question even before I asked it.

"Yes, sir," he said, "they like to ride—but don't like to push."

Something of the same is true of the person who rides around looking for unexpired time on a parking meter with a desire to park on some other fellow's nickel.

In a larger sense, this is true of church members who are not doing their part in funding the missions, education, and benevolent causes of our world. "They like to ride, but they don't like to push."

One noted church leader said, in reflecting on those who claim to be a part of the work and yet fail to support it: "I don't mind having these folks ride in the car, but if they're going to ride with us, they need to put some gas in the tank."

That's well said. There are those who need to learn to enjoy "pushing and giving" as much as riding.

That Is Awesome!

Teenagers often make use of the word "awesome" to describe almost anything unusual that happens.

However, most of us who are pastors or who have served as pastors can find many instances of that which is really awesome within the area of church work. For example:

Awesome is when the church auditorium on Sunday night is "comfortably filled"—meaning there is room for everybody to stretch out on the pew and take a nap!

Awesome is when the preacher throws himself into his sermon, gives it everything he has—only to have one of his church members come up after the service and say, without blinking an eye, "Preacher, that sermon was like water to a drowning man!"

Furthermore, in the same arena of comment, awesome is when one of the dear ladies of the congregation corners the preacher following the benediction and blurts out, "I just can't tell you how much your sermons have meant to my husband since he lost his mind!"

Awesome is when the pastor looks around the auditorium and says to himself, "This is one of the smallest Sunday night crowds we have had"—and then realizes that it is actually Sunday morning!

Awesome is when a deacon sees the pastor on the street and says, "I started to come to prayer meeting last week, but I wasn't sure you were still having it on Wednesday night!"

Awesome is when the minister announces his resignation, and one of the good women of the church comes up to say, "I'm sorry you're leaving"—to which the pastor modestly replies, "Oh, I'm sure when I'm gone the church will call somebody far better than me"—and the lady quickly responds, "Yes, that's what they said the last time!"

Now that is awesome!

Now Is the Time

I don't believe in procrastination. I cannot go along with those who seem to be comfortable in saying "Never do today that which you can put off until tomorrow."

The fact is, no matter how late the hour, I will not leave the office until my desk is clear.

Why do I choose this approach to my work? Please understand this: it means far more than a continuing attempt at being self-disciplined, well-organized, and efficient.

Good stewardship of time is involved, and furthermore, I learned long years ago that procrastination is a kind of self-sabotage.

It sabotages you, your work, and what you really want to do with your life.

Procrastination is a form of self-deception. "I could have gotten the job done," someone says, "if I had just had more time." That is self-deception.

In God's system of time, we have all been given days, weeks, and years containing the same number of hours. It is how we use the hours that is important. What we do with our time is what separates the achiever from the procrastinator.

The obvious dividing line between success and failure can be wrapped up in five words: "I did not have time."

For of all sad words of tongue or pen,
The saddest are these: "It might have been."

Procrastination is the enemy.

He was going to be all that God wanted him to be—tomorrow.

She was going to mean much to her church and the Lord's work—tomorrow.

Sadly for many, tomorrow never comes. For this reason, there is daily urgency about what we do in the service of God.

Jesus said, "I must work the works of him that sent me while it is day, for the night cometh when no man can work."

Procrastination must be put aside in favor of a recognition of this truth: "Today is the day of salvation." Now is the time.

Say Something Good

I was privileged to know and remember only one of my grandmothers. A small, rather delicate little lady, she was big of heart and spirit.

I don't think I have ever known any other person who so exemplified the Christian spirit as did she in her daily living.

I know she influenced my life—and the lives of others with whom she came in contact.

Her motto was: "If you can't say something good about somebody, don't say anything at all."

With many in our day, this is reversed. If they can't think of something bad to say about another person, they will wait until they can come up with a criticism or an insult that seems suitable for the occasion.

As the story goes, the minister was conducting a funeral service for the meanest man in town.

"It's customary," said the minister, "at this point in the service to say something good about the deceased. Is there anyone who would like to speak?"

No one in the congregation spoke up—or for that matter even looked as if he or she wanted to speak.

The minister tried again. "Now come on. You people are just not getting into the spirit of the service. I know he wasn't the nicest fellow in the world, but surely someone has a kind word to say about him."

The silence continued. The minister was aggravated as he said, "Now, we can't bury this man unless somebody has a good word for him."

Finally, from the back of the room, a little woman raised her hand and spoke out, "Well, his brother was even meaner!"

Be that as it may, let us each try to make our corner of the world a more pleasant place by saying something good.

A Mother's Kind of Love

In the play *A Raisin in the Sun*, there is a wonderful scene in which the mother is trying to teach her daughter what genuine love really is.

This is a struggling black family living on Chicago's southside with little hope of climbing out of poverty. The father dies and leaves a small insurance policy to his wife and children.

The mother has dreams of moving out of their "project" home and envisions a new start. The son, however, wants to use the money to go into business with a friend.

The mother reluctantly agrees to give the money to her son, but the deal falls through, and all the money is lost. They are left penniless, and the boy's sister is furious and launches a verbal attack on him.

The mother intercedes: "Daughter," she says, "I told you to love your brother."

"Love him," exclaimed the girl, "There ain't nothing left to love!"

The mother responds, "Daughter, there's always something left to love. If you ain't learned that, you ain't learned nothing."

"But Mama," protested the girl, "he lost everything."

"No, understand this, child. When do you think is the time to love somebody most? When he has done well and made things easy for everybody? That's not the time at all. The time to love him is when he's at his lowest cause the world has whipped him!"

"But Mama, . . . " the daughter offered.

"No, child," the mother declared, "In my house, there will be love!"

That is a Christian kind of love, that is God's kind of love, and that is a mother's love.

It Can Be Done

There are those who move through life believing that the circumstances never justify optimism.

They live by the words "It can't be done." For them, skepticism is a way of life.

More often than not, these are good and well-meaning people, but they dwell more on the impossible than the possible.

In 1870 the Methodists in Indiana were holding their annual conference.

At one point, the president of the college where they were meeting said, "I think we live in a very exciting age. I believe we are coming into a time of great inventions. I believe that one of these days men will fly through the air like birds."

"This is heresy," the Bishop told him. "The Bible says that flight is reserved for the angels. We will have no such talk here!"

After the conference, the Bishop, whose name was Wright, went home to be greeted by his two sons, Orville and Wilbur.

Many times our eyes are closed to the possibilities right on our own doorsteps.

Other times we get comfortable in our own ruts and refuse to consider other possibilities. A case in point was the grandmother who was asked by her granddaughter, "Granny, when they start taking regular space flights to the moon, are you going to make the trip?"

"No, honey," she answered, "I am going to stay home and watch television like the good Lord intended us to do."

Let us be certain that we keep our lives open to the possibilities. This requires an open mind, open heart, and open faith—a faith that swings wide to admit the possibilities.

The Scripture affirms this with the words "I can do all things through Christ who strengthens me." (Philippians 4:13)

It can be done.

You Make the First Move

The Sunday school teacher was telling her five-year-olds about the Golden Rule.

"Remember," she said to them, "We are here on earth to help others."

"Then," asked a little girl, "I want to know this—what are the others here for?"

Amazing, isn't it? How quickly children start sounding like adults.

Actually, there are too many of us who live as if we have forgotten, or, what is worse, never knew that the biggest and best game on earth is played by the Golden Rule.

It is the biggest game because the way it is played does not allow for littleness on the part of the players.

It is the best game because only the best of people play the game.

The rules of the game are simple—but not always easy to follow. Two or more can play at the same time.

But to begin the game in the right way, there is one thing you must remember: you move first.

Another interesting feature of the game is that you do not have to beat the other fellow to win. In the Golden Rule game, you win when you make a friend, and the only way you can make and hold a friend is by first being one. You move first.

This is a busy old world, and the people who win are the folks who have friendliness in their hearts and a sincere desire to help their neighbors.

The people who win the biggest blessings this world has to offer are living in accordance with the rules of the great Game of Life: "Do unto others as you would have them do unto you."

And remember the primary requirement of the game is this: you move first.

Conquering the Darkness

A power company mailed to its customers a pamphlet entitled, "What Should I Do if the Lights Go Out?"

Included were practical suggestions of procedures to follow in case of an emergency.

Fortunately, we as Christians have been given the secret of mastering the kind of darkness that is both life- and soul-threatening.

Looking forward to the coming of the Messiah, the prophet Isaiah said: "The people who walked in darkness have seen a great light; those who dwelt in a land of deep darkness, on them has light shined."

And when it did happen eight centuries later, John reported the experience in these words: "The light shines in the darkness, and the darkness has never put it out."

Our problem could be that we do not always see the light or allow it to illuminate our lives.

The story has it that the pupils of a wise and famous rabbi were much concerned about the existence of so much evil and darkness throughout the world. They asked him for a suggestion as to what they might do to rid the world of darkness. The rabbi told them they could start by sweeping the darkness out of a cellar with brooms.

Of course, this did not work. He then suggested they use sticks to beat the darkness into submission. This, too, was a futile effort.

Finally, his point clearly made, he urged them to meet the challenge of the darkness by lighting a candle.

Thus was the darkness dispersed.

We cannot sweep out or drive out the darkness, but we can conquer the darkness with a greater light—the Light of the world, Jesus Christ.

As John declared: "The light shines in the darkness, and the darkness has never put it out."

Looking on the Outward Appearance

USA Today published a story about a man named John Barrier, who, according to his own words, was treated "like I'd crawled out from under a rock" by the people in the bank.

Dressed in the rugged and soiled clothes of a construction worker, he had come into the bank to cash a small check.

After cashing the check at one teller's window, he started out of the bank—remembered his parking slip—and stopped to ask another teller to validate his parking ticket so that he could save the sixty-cent charge.

The teller, skeptical of him because of his appearance, refused to grant him that courtesy.

Surprised by this kind of treatment, John protested and the manager was summoned.

A discussion followed and, even though there seemed to be no good reason, the manager also refused to validate his parking slip.

Frustrated by the lack of courtesy shown him, John threatened to withdraw all of his funds from the bank. Again this was received with skepticism.

But the next day, to the surprise of both the manager and teller, John returned to the bank, withdrew his funds and closed his accounts, which totaled more than $2 million!

The bank president must have asked himself and his employees, What happened? Apparently, the bank employees had made the mistake of judging John's worth and importance by his appearance.

As the Scripture expresses it: "for man looks on the outward appearance, but the Lord looks on the heart." (1 Samuel 16:7)

It brings to mind the incident of the poorly dressed man who was brought into a medical center in serious condition.

Examining the old man, one doctor turned to another and said, "Well, let's see what we can do for this worthless bit of humanity."

Struggling to raise himself, the old man whispered these unexpected words, "Would you call worthless one for whom Christ died?"

From outward appearances, you cannot always tell where the treasure is.

Throw Out the Old

I have heard somewhere that in Rome, Italy, many people have the unusual habit of throwing something old out of the window on New Year's Eve.

If you happen to be walking along the street at this particular time, you might have an old discarded piece of furniture fall around you or on you.

According to an observer, they throw away old radios, television sets, and old clothes at the stroke of midnight.

Discarded items of all descriptions are tossed to the street with the idea of "down with the old."

Come to think of it, there would be great value in discarding certain other things from our lives on New Year's Eve.

For example, what about throwing out old resentments toward others? That would relieve many a person of a heavy burden.

If one would lighten and brighten his way into the New Year, let him toss away any resentment or ill feeling he holds against others.

How great it would be to get rid of all the old hatred and bitterness some harbor toward others.

In the finest sense of the word, that would usher in a blessed newness to replace old and burdensome problems.

The Scriptures have much to say about the importance of what is new.

Jesus said, "A new commandment I give unto you, that you love one another; as I have loved you, that you also love one another." (John 13:34)

The apostle Paul in writing to the Corinthians said, "Therefore if any man be in Christ, he is a new creation: old things are passed away; behold, all things are become new." (2 Corinthians 5:17)

If you would have a happy new year, remember this: Now is the time to throw out the old and bring in the new.

Playing the Game to Reach the Goal

Many years ago, as a young man in Macon, Georgia, my first assignment on the newspaper was as a sportswriter.

I enjoyed covering football, basketball, and baseball games, and other events connected with the world of sports.

True to life, many games are based on making goals.

In football and basketball, there are two goals, one at each end of the field or the court.

Both events have two teams, each choosing a goal and then dedicating themselves to defending it against the other team.

If a player on the football field becomes confused and runs toward the wrong goal, as has happened in a few recorded instances, the game can be lost.

The applied lessons for success in the larger game of life are obvious.

It is essential that all players have a clear picture in mind of the goals for which they are striving.

Even in the game of life, there are opposing forces that would seek to prevent you from crossing the goal line.

In the Christian life this is true, which makes it doubly important that we be certain of these things:

Know your goal, know where you want to go.

But be certain of this: one does not play the game alone. Many are on your team and are eager to see you meet your goal.

And of greater importance is this: the Lord is with you, and "He that is with you is greater than all who would oppose you."

You can reach the goal in the Christian life by remembering this: "If God be for us, who can be against us?"

Take a Careful Look

The wisdom of taking a long, careful look at the needs of our fellowman cannot be overemphasized.

In attempting to render assistance to others, we shall overlook a truth if we do not realize that things are not always what they appear to be on the surface.

One cannot understand the difficulties and hardships some people face without looking beneath the surface, standing in their shoes or experiencing their particular situations.

We must have hearts, ears, and eyes attuned to the needs of others or we shall miss many opportunities along the way to be of real assistance in meeting what are often desperate needs.

It was Christmas when a certain lady in the community joined a group of women distributing food baskets to the hungry.

At one house a woman with small children huddled near shook her head, and silently refused their offer of a turkey and a heavily loaded food basket with all of the necessities for a holiday feast.

Taken aback by her surprising refusal, several of the giftbearers were offended and felt that the apparently needy woman was ungrateful and had false pride.

"I was ready to drive away when something stopped me," one of the ladies said, and when she returned alone, she found the woman explaining to her children that their gas had been turned off. They had no way to cook the turkey, and so it was better for it to go to somebody who could cook it and enjoy it.

Of course, the lady took the turkey, cooked it, and returned it to the needy family, and left with a happy heart.

Be sure that you look carefully at the needs of your fellowman.

Don't Just Blow Your Horn—Do Something!

Those of us who spend a great deal of time on the expressways in bumper-to-bumper traffic often have the feeling that we are trapped on one long stagnant parking lot.

About the only thing that breaks the monotony is an occasional chuckle enjoyed from an amusing or discerning bumper sticker.

One thought-provoking bumper sticker offered this good advice: "Don't Honk—Push!"

All of us would have to admit that as we travel down the road of life, it is so much easier to honk than it is to help.

Anyone can blow a horn, but not many are willing to get out and push.

This applies also to church work. So things are not going smoothly in your church. Don't criticize. Pitch in and work to make things what they ought to be.

Attend. Participate. Get involved. Serve. Give.

You don't like the preacher? Pray for him. Lift him up. Don't put him down. Praise him.

Make certain that you do not become a member of the company of complainers.

Don't complain about your church. Instead, commit yourself to helping it carry out its mission.

Don't spend your time honking at your church's shortcomings. Instead, get behind it and push onward to greater achievement.

Don't waste your time blowing your horn—get behind every worthy Christian project and push with all the strength God has given you.

But Will We?

I was fortunate enough to grow up in a fine Christian home where Sunday was for church.

It was not an either/or matter. Our Baptist church was having Sunday School and worship services, and it never occurred to my parents that they could have church without us.

Now, for so many, the scene has changed.

The following attitudes toward worship are expressed by millions in our nation on any given Sunday:

"After all, we can worship God in our homes on Sunday morning." But do we?

"We can worship God in the woods and fields—and even on the golf course as well as we can in church." But do we?

"We don't belong to any one church. We feel that we can worship God in a different church each Sunday morning." But do we?

"We can feel just as worshipful in our lodge as we do in church." But do we?

"We can worship God by sending the children to Sunday School and staying home." But do we?

On a Sunday morning years ago in a resort community, this conversation was overheard as a family of four—mother, daddy, and two children—strolled past the church on their way to the beach.

The little girl spoke, "Daddy, can't we go to Sunday School and church?"

"Oh," replied the daddy, "we can worship just as well on the beach as we can in church."

The little girl's reply cut away all sham and pretense as she said, "But we won't, will we, Daddy?"

And in a word, that brings us down to the heart of the matter: We can, but will we?

An Inside Problem

The Great Wall of China is a sight to behold.

Visiting China while on a fact-finding tour of mission stations in Southeast Asia, we were astounded at the first glimpse of one of the Wonders of the World.

Hundreds of others who were there at the same time joined in the climbing of the Great Wall and marveled at the construction of what designers said was "an impenetrable fortress."

You recall that in ancient China, the people desired security from the barbaric hordes to the north; so they built the great Chinese wall.

It was so high they knew no one could climb over it and so thick that nothing could break it down.

And so, believing they were safe from all would-be attackers and that no harm could befall them, they settled down to enjoy what they perceived as real security.

But to their great surprise, China was invaded three times during the first years of the wall's existence.

Even more astonishing was the fact that not once did the invaders break through the wall or climb over the top. Each time they bribed a gatekeeper and then marched right through the gates.

The problem was an obvious one: the Chinese were so occupied with relying on the wall of stone that they forgot to teach their children integrity.

It seems there is a lesson here for all of us. We can be so guilty of concentrating on building walls that we neglect the inner fortress of the heart.

As the Bible says, "Keep thy heart with all diligence; for out of it are the issues of life." (Proverbs 4:23)

Let us make certain we are not so concerned with external security that we neglect the internal security of life.

For as the ancient Chinese discovered, we are much more likely to be destroyed from the inside than the outside.

Business Is Good

It doesn't take me very long to shop.

Like most men, I know what I want to buy. I go into the store, locate my intended purchase, and if I like it—and can afford it—I buy it.

Not so with my wife. She is one of the world's great department-store lookers. She can look for hours and never once open her pocketbook.

I have considered entering her in the "World Olympics for Store Lookers."

So, it naturally follows that when we go shopping together, I finish my shopping in a few minutes, find a vacant seat, and enjoy the passing scene.

Not too long ago, I sat in one of Atlanta's shopping malls and was fascinated by an old-fashioned organ grinder and his monkey. Even in my long years as a pastor, I have never seen anyone who was more effective at "taking the offering" than was the monkey.

Moving through the crowd, the monkey politely doffed his hat to every would-be contributor, received the offering, and moved on.

"I notice," I said to the organ grinder, "that when certain larger coins are dropped into his hat, the monkey applauds vigorously."

"Yes," replied the organ grinder, "that means business is good!"

Well, when our giving to worthy causes is what it ought to be, it also means that "business is good." It means that we are about "our Heavenly Father's business."

It means that we want to be good stewards of our possessions with which God has blessed us.

And it means something else: It means we care about missions. It means that we are concerned for the lost.

It means we care enough to give. And, in the finest sense, this does mean that "business is good!"

Ministerially Speaking

I was reading the other day of a minister who had printed the following all-inclusive calling card:

Name _____

Minister of _____ church

Elephants tamed.

Dragons slain.

Tigers trained.

Lost sheep found.

Counseling service (includes listening to sad stories).

Pilgrimages arranged.

Marriage ceremonies conducted.

Wars ended.

Lions fed.

Great cathedrals built.

The question suggested by this impressive list of duties is: What does he do in his spare time?

It could be that he may be like another clergyman I heard of who said: "I must confess that my besetting sin is exaggeration. But I do deplore it. In fact, I have prayed about it day and night for the last fifteen minutes!"

Surprisingly, this list of accomplishments on the calling card did not include one other item:

Lessons given on how to blow your own horn.

Or this:

Author of book: *My Wonderful Humility and How I Attained It.*

Don't Cool It—Warm It!

A popular expression of our day is "Cool it!"

But as is so often the case, we may be overdoing coolness.

Someone has said, "I'm horrified by the word 'cool.' Who wants to be cool? Coolness is an evasion of life. Being cool isn't being at all!"

Instead of cooling off, perhaps it would be better to warm up.

A well-known minister, writer, and lecturer says, "I keep a little sign on my desk as a daily reminder. It reads: 'Don't Lose the Luster.' "

But no matter how hard we try, we do at times lose a bit of the luster in our lives and in our attitudes. So it is important that we know how to restore the luster.

We can restore the luster in our lives by pausing to pray, to meditate, and to seek God's will and guidance.

We can bring back the luster by remembering to count our many blessings and, as the old hymn advises, "name them one by one, and it will surprise you what the Lord hath done."

The wonderful attitude of gratitude removes from our lives the dinginess of discouragement, the tarnish of pride, and the rust of resentment.

When we count our blessings, we add to the world's store of happiness and we multiply good will and harmony.

Moreover, we can restore the warmth and luster to our lives by forgetting ourselves in loving service to others.

So, here is a better idea: Don't cool it; warm up your life with new luster made brighter by the fuel of faith and strengthened by service to God and others.

Swap Whining for Praising

The town of Clio, Michigan, observed National Whiner's Day in connection with the day after Christmas when people usually return presents.

Although not aware that there is now set aside a national day for whiners, it was generally known that whining is a way of life for many. They belong to that large and dreaded group called the Company of Complainers.

I have known some who were so adept at whining and complaining that they could tell you good news and make you cry. They seem to overlook the scriptural warning: "And when the people complained, it displeased the Lord." (Numbers 11:1)

A case in point was the woman who, strangely, seemed to *enjoy* poor health. Said she, "I think I may feel a little better today, but I am afraid to say so because I know I am going to feel worse tomorrow."

True, there is enough sadness in the world to occupy our thoughts. But there is also enough gladness on which we may focus with praise and commitment.

And surely there would not be many among us who would deny that the great need of our day is to accentuate the positive and eliminate the negative.

Consider this. Even when we look into all the corners of life, how can we whine?

How can we whine? When we look up and see on the horizon of life Golgotha's hillside from which there rises, like a giant plus sign, the cross of Christ.

How can we whine? When we hear in the background the sound of nails being driven through flesh into that wooden cross.

How can we whine? When we hear from the lips of our Saviour the words "It is finished."

For the Christian, habitual whining is not a fitting response to Christ's sacrificial love. A better response is suggested in the words of Isaac Watts's beautiful old hymn:

Were the whole realm of nature mine,
That were a present far too small;
Love so amazing, so divine,
Demands my soul, my life, my all.

Thanksgiving Every Day

Thanksgiving is a favorite holiday of mine.

And it isn't just because of the eating, although I must admit that partaking of good food remains and ever shall be a much-preferred indoor and outdoor pastime.

Eating is part of my doctrine.

But Thanksgiving is important because it is a day when one pauses to reflect on how many good things have accompanied life.

Thanksgiving to God gives new power to daily living, opening the generators of the heart to receive joyfully and respond gratefully.

Our forefathers knew that self-centered as we are, we would need a time such as Thanksgiving to stop and think of the blessings of life.

Honest reflection moves us to realize that many blessings—as numerous as they are—have gone unnoticed.

An anonymous writer once shared these innermost feelings on Everyday Thanksgiving:

"Even though I clutch my blanket and growl when the alarm rings each morning, thank you, Lord, that I can hear. Some are deaf.

"Even though I keep my eyes tightly closed against the morning light as long as I can, thank you, ,Lord that I can see. Many are blind.

"Even though I huddle in my bed and put off the effort of rising, thank you, Lord, that I have the strength to rise. Many are bedridden.

"Even though my job is often trying, thank you, Lord, for the opportunity to work. There are many who have no work.

"And even though I grumble and bemoan my fate from day to day, I know I am blessed in many ways. Thank you, Lord, for the gift of life."

So, let us look up with gratitude, observing Thanksgiving not as a seasonal ceremony but a daily habit.

Looking Out of Brighter Windows

A little girl was crying her heart out as she stood looking out of the north window at her father as he buried her dead pet kitten.

The tears had started slowly at first. Then they filled her eyes, overflowed, and streamed down her cheeks.

She was sobbing when her grandpa came up behind her, reached out and gently placed his hand on her shoulder.

He patted her a few times, and then his kind old arm lovingly went around her.

"Come with me, child," he said, as he led her over to the east window of their home.

"You've been looking out of only one window," he continued, "I want you to look out of another window."

They stood together and viewed a new and different scene.

They saw a beautiful robin feeding its babies in the nest.

The blooming flowers in the yard were almost too beautiful to describe.

The little girl's tears were now stilled as she heard her grandfather say, "Always remember this: no matter what the circumstances may be, you must try to look out of the brighter windows of life."

Here is good advice for all of us.

Life would be more pleasant for all if we made a habit of looking out of the brighter windows.

Let's look through the window of concern for our fellowman.

And it is just as important that we look out of the window of understanding.

Furthermore, our view of life cannot begin to be all it should be unless we are willing to look through the window of love.

But the last word is that these brighter views are made possible by the all-important act of looking through the window of faith.

Can These Bones Live?

Ezekiel described his vision in this way: "The hand of the Lord was upon me, and he brought me out by the Spirit of the Lord, and set me down in the midst of the valley; it was full of bones. And he led me round among them; and behold, there were very many upon the valley; and lo, they were very dry. And he said to me, 'Son of man, can these bones live?' " (Ezekiel 37:1-3)

The vision of the prophet deals with dry bones that come alive. But although there are bones in most organizations and many churches, they do not always come alive.

For example, there are the *Wishbones*. They spend their time wishing that somebody else would get the job done. If wishing would make it so, they would enjoy unusual success.

Then we have the *Knucklebones*. They knock everything. No matter what it is, there is no point in discussing it. They are against it.

The next group could best be described as the *Jawbones*. They will do all the talking but very little else. They are willing to express themselves—but unwilling to exert themselves.

But fortunately, for the good of the church and the progress of the work, we have the *Backbones*. They are the ones who carry the load. You can count on them. While others are merely thinking about doing something, they are rolling up their sleeves and getting on with the task.

In all things, we can say, "Thank God for the Backbones."

With their help, these bones can live and the work of the church can go forward.

Keep On Keeping On

The approach of the national observance of Columbus Day brings the inspiring reminder of the indomitable spirit, courage, and tenacity of this great explorer. His was not an easy task to begin with—but it was made more difficult by members of the self-appointed bucket brigade who were quick to throw cold water on the project.

For weeks before Columbus discovered the New World, some members of his crew kept telling him, "Turn back before we run out of food and perish! Turn back before we sail off the edge of the world!"

There was a name for these people—*consultants*. And another name—*critics*. Every great project, every church, and every worthy convention endeavor needs team players.

Think of the possibilities: tackles, guards, centers. One pastor must have been thinking about football and the need for team play when he said of one of his members, "He's one of our drawbacks." To continue, to stay one's course in the face of such opposition ranks high on the ladder of courage.

In the poem by Joaquin Miller, Columbus heard this from his first mate:

"My men grow mutinous day by day;
What shall I say, brave admiral, say,
If we sight naught but seas at dawn?"
"Why, you shall say at break of day:
Sail on! Sail on! Sail on! And on!"

They sailed and sailed, as winds might blow,
Until at last the blanched mate said:
"Should I and all my men fall dead.
These very winds forget their way.
For God from these dread seas is gone.
Now speak, brave admiral, speak and say—"
He said: "Sail on! Sail on! And on!"

Then, pale and worn, he kept his deck
And peered through darkness—and then a speck—
A light! A light! A light! A light!
It grew to be Time's burst of dawn.
He gained a world; he gave that world
Its grandest lesson: "On! Sail on!"

It is a lesson for all who sail through troubled seas: Sail on!
Let's keep on keeping on and look for the light of a brighter day.

Costly Gifts

Shouting "Charge!" as they moved from store to store, early Christmas shoppers threw themselves into the task long before Thanksgiving. One department store suggested a way to keep Christmas with us all year long. "Buy things on our monthly payment plan," they advised.

It is interesting to watch determined shoppers who seem to know exactly what they want. As one young father said, "I just came back from Christmas shopping. I bought a TV game and an electric train." Then he added, "And I also got something for the children."

Still, it must be said that in most cases the true spirit of Christmas giving does shine through.

In one comic strip, the younger sister is rejoicing as she tells her big brother, "Look, I got nine dollars and eleven cents to spend on Christmas presents!"

But the brother replies, "You can't buy something for everyone with nine dollars and eleven cents!"

But with supreme assurance and commitment, the sister declares, "I'm going to do my best!"

Walking away, the older brother douses her good intentions with the cold water of sarcasm as he answered, "Well, they are certainly going to be cheap presents!"

But the determined sister reminds us of the true meaning of Christmas as she says, "Nothing is cheap if it costs everything you have!"

Thus we are reminded that nothing is cheap about Christmas as God sees it, for, after all, he gave us everything he had in the gift of his Son.

As Christmas approaches, the newspaper advertisements will offer all kinds of gift suggestions.

But the fact remains that a loving God has given to each of us who trust in him life's supreme gift—the gift of salvation through his Son, Jesus Christ.

Good Advice to All
for the Living of These Days

Here are some very practical down-to-earth rules for living in these troubled days. We would do well to heed these Rules for Survival:

(1) "If you open it, close it." This could apply to most anything—but it could be most appropriately applied to the mouth. In this day, when there's too much talk and too little silence, if you open your mouth, don't forget to close it.

(2) "If you turn it on, turn it off." This is wise counsel—especially if "it" refers to criticism. If you turn it on, please remember to turn it off.

(3) "If you break it, repair it." There might be less destructive behavior in this cantankerous old world if the requirement was that one repairs whatever one breaks.

(4) "If you borrow it, return it." Why, if nothing else, this payback of what is owed would improve world economy. After all, the Bible instructs us to "owe no man."

(5) "If you make a mess, clean it up." Even though this may sound like parental advice to an untidy child, this is a word needed by all "children"—both young and old. Some have recklessly made a mess of life as we once knew it and have done so with no thought of cleaning it up. The mess-uppers and clean-uppers ought to be the same persons.

(6) "If you don't know how to operate it, leave it alone." Too much of the machinery of the world is now being run by those who have little or no idea of what they are doing.

They are like the five-year-old who got into a large truck, released the brake and ran into a highway barricade. He got it started, but didn't know how to stop it.

(7) "If it doesn't concern you, don't mess with it." That's another good way of saying, "mind your own business." But there's something else. The boy Jesus said, "I must be about my *Father's* business."

The point well taken is that we, too, must be about *our Father's* business—not the business of someone else.

Real Love

These were not easy words spoken by Jesus: "A new commandment I give to you, that you love one another; even as I have loved you, that you also love one another. By this all men will know you are my disciples, if you have love for one another." (John 13:35)

No doubt about it. Jesus was talking about real love. The genuine article.

Over the years I have not always welcomed the saccharin and artificial sweetener suggestion that all we needed to do was just "love everybody and everything would turn out all right."

This overlooks two facts: one, life isn't that simple; and two, some people are terribly hard to love.

Moreover, some who offer the glib generality to "love everybody" may not have the slightest notion of what love really is.

They may confuse it with a warm glow which could just as easily be a high temperature resulting from a bad cold.

Love, according to Jesus, is very real and very costly. It is never halfhearted. It is love without reservation.

Of this kind of love, the apostle Paul said, "Love is patient and kind; love is not jealous or boastful; it is not arrogant or rude. Love does not rejoice in the wrong, but rejoices in the right. Love bears all things, hopes all things, endures all things."

Love is not easy. It is not simple. It is not cheap. It has a high price tag attached. But it is essential if we are to make the journey with our Lord who said, "By this all men will know you are my disciples if you have love for one another."

Worthwhile Remembrance

When viewed from the right perspective, the observance of Memorial Day can be more of a holy day than a holiday.

It is always profitable for followers of Christ who have embraced the Christian faith to remember the rock from which they were hewn.

We owe a great debt of gratitude to our spiritual forefathers who as pioneers of the faith blazed a trail of dedication and commitment, which established the sturdy foundation on which we stand.

The work and witness of others must be remembered as we think of their personal contributions to our spiritual pilgrimage.

Remember and be grateful for faithful pastors—those who have led countless numbers to Christ and also continued to nurture and grow up their converts in the faith.

Say a prayer of thanksgiving for dedicated Sunday School teachers who made Christ real to you through their Bible teaching.

Reflect on loving parents whose heart's desire was that you, their child, become all that God wanted you to be.

Recall Christian friends who offered a loving fellowship which, by any measurement, is something akin to a little bit of heaven on earth.

As we remember, we shall acknowledge that we owe a debt to many, for gratitude can be defined as the loving memory of the heart.

We can ill afford to forget the past, for gratitude in the present results from remembering all that was done in bygone days.

This kind of remembrance is always worthwhile.

Hats off in respect and appreciation, for what has been done in the past can prompt us to roll up our sleeves for the work at hand and thereby with diligence assure a victorious march into the future.

Huggers Needed

Returning from a speaking engagement at a South Georgia missions conference, I switched on my car radio and heard a woman making an appeal for volunteers to assist with a track meet for retarded and handicapped children.

"We could use," she said, "a large number of 'huggers'—persons who would wait at the finish line to hug the children and tell them they had done great!"

As I drove along through the rolling hills of Middle Georgia, I could not get rid of that thought.

Wanted—Huggers. There would be good reason to place this appeal in the want-ad section of every newspaper: Huggers Needed.

For it seems that so many who are now running the difficult races of life could benefit from having someone waiting at "the finish line" to reach out to them and speak the needed word of encouragement, "You've done a good job."

Bumper stickers now ask the important question: "Have You Hugged Your Child Today?"

It is an important question that deserves the right answer.

Needless to say, life would, for everyone, run more smoothly if bolstered by the strength of genuine encouragement, affection, and appreciation.

So may each of us resolve to make that extra effort to encircle others with the gift of love.

This act of concern could turn out to be for many the sweetest music this side of heaven. In fact, it could bridge the gap between now and the hearing of the Master's final word, "Well done, good and faithful servant."

In the meantime, as the woman said in her appeal, "Huggers are needed."

Under New Management

As one who likes to eat, I am not that hard to please with food. I like everything that is put before me.

In fact, I could join with the fellow who said, "The worst food I ever had was wonderful."

This was not true, however, with a man described by Randall Runcon who went into a certain restaurant and was sorely disappointed by the meal.

The food was cold and poorly prepared, and the restaurant was dirty.

The table had not been wiped off. If the busboy had done anything, he must have limited his activity to rearranging the grease.

When the man complained about the food, the waitress was surly and discourteous, and the owner seemed not to care.

Finally, his patience exhausted, the man left, saying, "I will never eat in this restaurant again!"

But a couple of months later, the man passed by, saw a sign in the window, and so he went in and enjoyed a marvelous meal. The food was perfect, and the restaurant was immaculate, with the floor now cleaner than the table had been before. The waitress was prompt and had a pleasant disposition.

And the owner thanked him for his business and said if anything at all was wrong to please let him know. Furthermore, he said that the most important thing was the satisfaction of his customers. Of course, the man left assuring the owner that he would be back soon and often.

What made the difference? It was the sign in the window. It read: "Open—Under New Management."

Oftentimes life is like that restaurant in its first condition—dirty, surly, unpleasant, and unsatisfying. What can make a difference? What can change all that?

Actually, one thing. Over the window of that messed-up, misdirected life there must be placed a very important sign that reads: "Under New Management."

As the apostle Paul said, "Therefore, if any man be in Christ, he is a new creature: old things are passed away; behold, all things are become new." (2 Corinthians 5:17)

What's Wrong with This Woman?

A Nashville, Tennessee, newspaper published a feature story about a Mrs. Craig, eighty-one, who had not missed church in 1,040 Sundays or a total of twenty years of perfect attendance.

Hasn't missed church in twenty years? Why, you could accuse this good lady of being unorthodox.

If news of this gets around to the right people, they will surely call for a special investigation.

After all, there are too many unanswered questions about this lady.

(1) Doesn't Mrs. Craig ever have company visiting her on Sunday? Or is she so dedicated to her church that when she has company she is bold enough to say, "You folks can go with me or make yourself at home—I'm going to church!"

(2) Doesn't she ever go out on Saturday night and find herself so tired on Sunday morning that she just can't make it to church?

(3) Doesn't a lady of her advanced age have nervous spells when she gets in a crowd? Or doesn't she catch cold, have headaches and that aching, run-down feeling? (A condition that for some is made even worse by attending church.)

(4) And what about the Sunday evening service? Didn't she want to stay home and watch TV?

(5) Doesn't she ever choose to stay in bed on Sunday morning when it rains, snows, or gets too hot or cold in Nashville?

(6) Hasn't she ever become angry or "put out" with her minister or a fellow church member and decided she would just "show them" by staying away?

(7) And hasn't she at some point in the twenty years felt unappreciated and wanted to stay home and bathe in self-pity?

These questions need to be answered. And who knows? When the investigation is completed, it may be found that Mrs. Craig is guilty of coming down with a good case of religion many years ago—a condition made more permanent by the fullness of her love for the Lord and her church.

Honesty and Truth

I love music, but not all of it. Some present-day music threatens to break into a tune, but never does.

Traveling across Georgia, I often punch station selector buttons with the vain hope of coming across a few hours of good listening.

One night the band was heavy on brass and drumbeat, but in the midst of all the loud noise, there came the poetic words: "Honesty is a lonely word, one that's almost never heard."

Honesty is becoming more difficult to find in our everyday life. For example, the front doorbell rings. A mother grabs her seven-year-old and whispers: "Go to the door and tell whoever it is that no one is home."

This gives the child a poor concept of honesty and truth.

Honesty and truth in all of our dealings with everyone would improve the quality of life.

In a play by Channing Pollock, Archie comes home tired and beat. He has been down at city hall trying to stand against the pressures of the councilmen to do an unethical thing concerning a proposed housing project.

Archie would not give in. He was told by the men who despised him because he would not cooperate that he was a little man.

Now seated beside Jennifer, his wife, he says, "I'm not a big man."

Jennifer asks, "What's a big man, Archie?"

He answers, "Oh, I guess somebody like Henry Ford."

Jennifer says, "No, Archie, a big man is a man who keeps his soul!"

This is well said. Be honest. Be truthful. Keep your word. Hold on to your Christian principles. Keep your soul.

Trusting God

It was many years ago. I was a student pastor at Southeastern seminary. One deacon in my church was a quiet, unassuming man who worked hard and had built up vast holdings of land and other possessions.

However, he never entertained the thought of tearing down his barns to build bigger barns and sitting back and saying, "Soul, take your ease. Eat, drink, and be merry."

Fact is, he worked every day of his life. If you saw him on the street, you would see a man in overalls with the sweat of labor on his brow. He and his wife had started with just a few acres of land, and they had worked hard. They stayed close to God and close to each other.

In twenty years he was a large landholder, owned two hotels, and had other real estate and large accounts in banks and savings institutions.

He was a simple man, uneducated, but wise and spiritually mature. One day, in a quiet moment, we were talking about all he had accumulated through the years. With a trace of tear in his eyes, he said, "I owe it all to God. God and I have always had a system. When I got my first little plot of land, after I had plowed with a mule and planted, I got under a shade tree, took off my hat, bowed my head, and talked to God."

He said, "I don't believe I ever planted a crop I did not commit to God in prayer and then share with Him the firstfruits of all I harvested."

If we follow the same system: doing the best we can, trusting God for results and then committing to God the firstfruits of all we harvest, then we, too, can move forward, not only in stewardship, but in every area of our Lord's work.

Say What You Mean

Failing to communicate may be among the leading problems of our day.

Truth is, if we cannot communicate, we cannot negotiate.

Moreover, if we cannot communicate, we cannot cooperate.

It was encouraging to read that language expert Edwin Newman has said, "Pompous, incomprehensible language could be on the decline."

From time to time, most of us have been either baffled or bored by the windy jargon in contracts, legal documents, or other formal communications.

Newman describes this kind of lingo as words that "groan with false dignity."

Instead of communicating in sharp, easy-to-understand language that says exactly what the words mean, some writers seek to disguise thoughts in strange costumes of confusion that expand them beyond recognition.

Bad debts are plainly and simply bad debts, but, as described by banks, they become "nonperforming loans."

And although every schoolboy knows that cowboys are cowboys, one government department labeled them as "mobile mountain-range technicians."

When you fly, the flight attendant does the same thing in an attempt to reassure passengers by describing life preservers under the seats as "personal flotation devices."

It must be confessed that clergymen are also guilty of using bloated language that adds to the difficulty of understanding great spiritual truths.

A case in point is the young boy who, because of the illness of his mother, went alone to the worship service where the preacher launched his vocabulary into the upper altitudes for a good forty-five minutes before finally coming down to earth just in time for the benediction.

Returning home, the son was asked by his mother, "Well, what did the preacher preach on?"

In truth, the boy replied, "He never did say."

The Train Rolls On

Several centuries ago, near the close of his life, William Penn, the governor of Pennsylvania, was caught in a sordid and humiliating experience.

It was trouble enough to try the soul of any man. In fact, most men would have broken under the burden, but Penn refused to be discouraged. Throughout the entire distressing experience, he remained serene, calm, confident, and unafraid.

One of his friends described this unusual victory of his over contrary circumstances.

"The more he is pressed," declared his friend, "the more he rises. He has the spirit to bear up under difficulty. His foundation remains."

These words are pertinent today, for anyone who is going to live triumphantly in these chaotic times needs the capacity to bear up under difficulty.

Each day seems to have its own crisis, and trouble for many is on the daily menu.

The important question to emerge from all of this is: Are we equal to the demands now before us?

If we answer truthfully, the reply must be: No, we are not equal to all the demands of this day. But God is.

As the Scripture says, "In all these things, we are more than conquerors through Him that loved us."

Our sure foundation must stand on Christ as we choose faith over fear. He is our strength. He is our Rock, and he brings the victory.

Knowing this, and practicing the way of faith, it is possible to choose the courageous way.

With the Lord's inner strength, his servants can move against opposition and criticism.

As the old courthouse square commentator once said, "The true leader with faith keeps moving on in spite of everything.

"After all," he said, "a rolling train don't stop for no barking dog!"

You Are What You Swallow

Perhaps in this day, more than in other days, a man can be measured by what claims his attention.

These are pertinent questions: Who and what do you listen to?

Will you swallow anything? Some persons will, you know.

British surgeons removed two spoons, four coins, several pieces of wire and a bedspring from the stomach of a young man.

How could one swallow all of this? That's a good question—but no more than the question of how supposedly intelligent persons can swallow idle gossip, unfounded rumors, half-truths, and harsh criticism of others!

Moreover, there are many other persons who are just as quick to absorb every pessimistic report and cynical observation that comes their way.

Nutritionists, I am told, claim that "we are what we eat."

And the Bible declares, "As a man thinketh in his heart, so is he." (Proverbs 23:7)

It all comes down to this: be careful what you swallow.

Ask yourself these questions: Is it true? Is it helpful? Will it hurt or help all those concerned?

Watching what you swallow may help you avoid a bad case of indigestion and the usual remorse and regret that goes with the mournful admission: "I can't believe I ate the whole thing!"

It Is a Good Thing to Give Thanks

We should not wait for Thanksgiving season to be reminded that "It is a good thing to give thanks." (Psalm 92:1)

Failing to express appreciation and show gratitude is a neglected virtue of our day. In our day-to-day journey through life, we are prone to forget that everyone hungers for appreciation. It is the legal tender that everyone enjoys.

Two of the brightest words in our language are the two simple words, "Thank you."

It is a good thing to give thanks to others. That thoughtful father was right when he called his son aside and said, "Listen, son, mother sometimes gets tired like all mothers do. Don't forget to thank her."

Love mixed with gratitude and appreciation makes some of the best medicine one can take, and it is a sure cure for that run- down feeling of not being appreciated.

Furthermore, it is a good thing to give thanks unto the Lord for all of His blessings. And there is always something for which to be grateful.

A very disturbed man once said, "I don't have anything to be thankful for: I owe so many bills, and I can't pay any of them."

"Well," replied his friend, "just be thankful you aren't one of your creditors."

And no matter what our circumstances may be, there is always something to be thankful for. A minister once preached to a tightfisted congregation in a small community.

When they took the offering, they decided to just pass the preacher's hat, which came back absolutely empty. Bowing his head for the offertory prayer, the preacher said, "I thank Thee, Lord, that I got my hat back."

Unlike this dear brother, many of us have been abundantly blessed, and we need to be thankful and grateful for the love and blessings of God.

Let us vow on Thanksgiving Day to return the joy of gratitude and appreciation to their rightful places in our hearts.

Then, we shall come to realize what the Psalmist meant when he said: "It is a good thing to give thanks unto the Lord"—and to others.

The Look of Faith

It was my privilege in recent months to be the speaker during revival services in one of our fine Georgia churches.

A growing, progressive city with warmhearted friendly people made my stay a pleasant one. To be associated with a dedicated pastor and people is the finest fellowship this side of heaven.

On the final day of the scheduled revival services, the pastor asked me to join him in visiting two members of his church who recently had legs amputated.

One gentleman, now eighty-five, had lost a leg, was fitted with an artificial limb, and went back to driving his pickup truck.

Some of God's children always seem to possess an indomitable spirit. No matter what happens, they retain the look of faith—the upward look.

The next visit was to the home of a man who had both legs amputated.

He spends his time, the pastor says, phoning people, encouraging others to keep the faith through all of life's trials and tribulations.

When it was time to leave, the pastor and I stood to join hands with this brother for a word of prayer.

With tongue in cheek, the man looked up from his wheelchair and said, "You will excuse me for not getting up."

A sense of humor, great faith, and commitment to the cause of Christ will assure the upward look.

No matter how dark the situation may be as we pass through life, the path is always made brighter by the look of faith.

Is Your Foot on the Oxygen Hose?

Even when people mean well, they can at times create more problems than they can solve.

One young inexperienced pastor was at the hospital visiting an elderly member of his church. Thoughtlessly he sat down on the side of her bed and loudly inquired into the nature of her surgery.

It went on like this until finally he said, "Before I leave, is there anything else I can do for you?"

To that, the sweet-spirited lady replied, "Well, you could take your foot off my oxygen hose."

This kind of behavior is excused by some who say, "Oh, anyway he is sincere," when the fact is that one can be sincere and at the same time sincerely wrong.

The forward progress of our churches would be enhanced by the willingness of all to concentrate more on the possibilities that challenge us than the problems that beset us.

Surely we can see the wisdom of forgetting the mistakes of the past and pressing on to greater achievements of the future. And every person should recognize the value of giving so much time to the improvement of oneself that you have no time to criticize others.

Well-intentioned but wrong actions have a way of "standing on the oxygen hose" and cutting off the breath of fresh air so desperately needed by any worthy endeavor.

A good question to consider is this: Are you, by your actions, stifling the enthusiasm of others?

Are you breathing new life into the work by possibility thinking or smothering the work with problem thinking?

As the lady in the hospital said, "There is one other thing you can do—take your foot off the oxygen hose."

Looking Up — Jim N. Griffith   149

Cast Your Cares

As someone has said, "Life is just one thing after another."

But in today's world, it often turns out to be one disturbing thing after another.

Still, the light shining through all of this is found in the Scripture: "Be anxious for nothing, but in everything by prayer and supplication with thanksgiving, let your requests be made known unto God. And the peace of God, which passeth all understanding, shall keep your hearts and minds through Christ Jesus." (Philippians 4:6,7)

Be anxious for nothing. Don't worry about anything. That sounds strange in our world where insecurity seems to saturate our society.

And yet, this scriptural statement stands. Don't be anxious about anything! But how do we keep this command?

Certainly it does not mean to be careless or thoughtless. The answer is not in our weakness, but in God's strength. This is the way to peace.

Peter, in his first epistle, writes: "Casting all your care [all your anxiety] upon him; for he careth for you." (1 Peter 5:7)

F. B. Meyer said: "Two things come between our souls and unshadowed fellowship with God: sin and care."

Brooding over the past, disturbed by the present, and dwelling on what *might* happen is a common fault with many.

The world says in a feeble way: "Do your best to stop worrying."

Peter's word from God is much better: "Casting all your care upon him; for he careth for you."

Or as one great old Christian warrior said: "Lord, help me to remember that there ain't nothing that you and me together can't handle."

The Power of Love

Truth is, we do not need Valentine's Day to remind us of the world's desperate need for love.

As the wise old professor once said, "If you want a verb to conjugate, you cannot do better than to take the verb, 'to love'."

There are people who are quick to say that, for some reason—they can't exactly say why—they don't like a certain person.

Take, for example, the verse written on an Oxford University wall by a student concerning one of his professors:

I do not like thee, Dr. Fell,
The reason why I cannot tell;
But this alone I know full well,
I do not like thee, Dr. Fell.

But the fact is, "to love or not to love" cannot be a question for a Christian, according to Jesus.

Love, Jesus said, is the Christian's "identification card."

A retired minister stood before a pastor's conference and said, "If I am ever tempted to doubt my salvation, I am comforted that I have at least one mark of a Christian, namely, that I love my brethren."

Our Lord said, "By this shall all men know that ye are my disciples, if ye have love one to another." (John 13:35)

This kind of love is not theory; it is life. It is not academic; it is dynamic. It is not mere talk; it is deeds.

A dirty, cursing, drunken man disrupted a bookstore in a middle American city. Asked by missionary Clark Scanlon what he wanted, the man cried, "I want somebody to love me."

In that moment, Mr. Scanlon's attitude changed. "I realized," Mr. Scanlon said, "God could give me the power to love someone different from all my concepts of cleanliness and moral standards. I loved this man because of what he could become in Christ."

Such is the power of love.

Daddy Practiced What Others Preached

The observance of Father's Day has never received the center stage and same bright spotlight as has Mother's Day.

The loving "hand that rocked the cradle" may not have always "ruled the world"—but a mother's touch has been felt wherever life has been lived to the fullest and finest degree.

However, the importance of the role of the father cannot be overlooked. Indeed, the saying must be more than "It's father who pays." In the Christian household the byword must be "It is father who prays."

Shakespeare said, "It is a wise father that knows his own child."

And the father who prays with and for his children shall know them and their full potential.

One added advantage of this familiarity is that the child shall also know and appreciate the best about his father.

I read with amusement this Father's Day note sent to his dad by a young boy: "Dear Dad: Happy Father's Day! I don't care what mommy says—I think you are the best father in the whole world. Love, Your Son."

And then there was the note from a daughter to her father: "Dear Father: I wouldn't love you any more if you were the richest man in the world, but it sure would help. Your Loving Daughter."

Be that as it may, one cannot deny that the good and godly father is an excellent role model for his children.

As one dad expressed it, "I'm no model father. All I'm trying to do is live so that when people tell my son he reminds them of me, he'll stick out his chest instead of his tongue."

Proclaim magazine sums it all up for us with the incident of the young boy who was asked, "Under whose preaching were you converted?"

"Oh, it wasn't under anybody's preaching—it was under my daddy's practicing."

How to Be Miserable

Happiness is much preferred over misery, and I am concerned with presenting the way to the happy life.

But it is possible to put over a positive truth with a negative thought.

Here are the ways to be miserable:

Think only of yourself. Talk about yourself. Let it be known that you have a bad case of "I"-strain.

Always expect to be appreciated.

Insist upon special treatment and consideration.

Be jealous and envious of others. If anything good happens to someone else, pout about it.

Demand that everyone agree with your opinion on anything. If someone dares to disagree, sulk about it and drive off in your huffmobile.

Shirk your duties and then blame others when work is not done.

Focus all attention on yourself and your needs.

Do as little as possible for others. Be selfish.

Love yourself supremely.

It is true. You can do all these things and be perfectly miserable.

But you can choose another way and find joy.

Jesus said, "He that would keep his life shall lose it, but he that would lose his life for my sake shall find it."

Again, Jesus said, "I came not to be served, but to serve."

And our Lord offered the key to the good life in these words: "He that shall be the greatest of all shall be the servant of all."

Unselfishness, thinking of others, and seeking to serve God and man.

Do these things, and happiness shall be your reward.

True Friends Are True Treasures

As one grows older and gains some wisdom with the passing of the years, it becomes easier to recognize that true friends are true treasures.

The emphasis here is on *true* friends, not "fair-weather friends" who are here today and gone tomorrow.

Great friends are great blessings and are worthy of all appreciation. For true friendship endures.

I agree with the statement: "I do not give my friendship lightly, but once it is given it is never withdrawn."

What is a true friend? Here are a few descriptions of true friendship.

A friend is a source of gladness—even when there is not too much to be happy about.

A friend can make your grief less painful and your pain more bearable.

A friend eases your disappointment and makes your problems easier to solve.

But a friend is even more than this.

A friend rejoices with you when you soar to the brightness of the mountaintops and then solemnly walks beside you through the darkness of the valley.

A friend is one with whom you are always comfortable and one for whom you are ever grateful.

A friend is one who lifts you up and never puts you down.

As one great man replied, when asked why he had enjoyed such great success in life, "I had a friend."

This statement is easy to understand when one knows from personal experience that a friend is one who strengthens you with his prayers, blesses you with his love, and encourages you with his faith and hope.

A true friend is an earthly treasure who brings to your life one of the great joys this side of heaven.

Attend Church in Person!

When we move through the cold, inclement weather of winter, it would be well to remind ourselves of the importance of faithfulness in church attendance.

It should be noted that the empty pew often speaks loudly of our lack of commitment and dedication to the worship service.

With so many businesses now remaining open on Sunday, along with various recreational activities which dominate the day, worship is frequently squeezed from the schedule of many would-be churchgoers.

Once, in answer to a query about the necessity of working on Sunday, evangelist Billy Graham declared, "It should not detract from a man's reverence to do what is required. Even Jesus spoke about the ox in the ditch on the sabbath. But if your ox gets in the ditch every sabbath, you should either get rid of the ox or fill up the ditch."

This is good advice. I also like Calvin Coolidge's pointed answer to the question, "Can't I worship God just as well out in the green open fields?"

His reply was characteristically brief and brusque, "You can, but you don't!"

Like all such terse statements, it does not take exceptions into account, but it goes to the root of the matter.

There is an undeniable truth to be gleaned from this little verse:

Whenever I go past a church,
I always stop to visit;
So, at last when I'm carried in,
Folks won't ask, "Who is it?"

The latter may be too often the case with many. In a small mountain village in Kentucky a young minister made this somewhat unusual funeral announcement from his pulpit: "The funeral of John Brown will be held from this church tomorrow at 3 p.m., and Mr. Brown will be here himself, in person, for the first time in several years."

Worshiping in person is the way to go, now and at the last.

Closet Christians

As the story goes, a noted philosopher and educator became upset and suddenly left a discussion group at a tea quite disgusted, slamming the door behind him.

One person, attempting to relieve the tension resulting from this embarrassing turn of events, remarked, "Well, he has gone."

To this the hostess replied, "No, he hasn't. That's a closet!"

The guest who made this rash and senseless blunder joined company with all those who have committed the error of barking up the wrong tree, turning down a blind alley, or, surprise of all surprises, mistaking a closet for an outside door.

This incident is something of a commentary on our times. In anger, some rush down the wrong road, only to discover too late that there is no way out.

The Bible has a word for it: "There is a way which seemeth right to a man, but the end thereof is the way of destruction." (Proverbs 14:12)

Then, there are others who, at the smallest provocation are quick to go off in a swivet.

Like the man who rushed in to the closet by mistake, they have a short and unsatisfactory trip.

And we share the same plight when we attempt to rush from God's presence and find that we are confined to ourselves.

For in truth, he who is confined with an angry self soon learns that he is in the company of a very hostile companion.

The world—even our little part of it—has so many desperate needs that the whole complicated process of life would be better served if some of us would follow this simple suggestion:

Next time you feel angry and "rush into a closet"—let it be your prayer closet.

The Joy of Giving

The fault I find hardest to take in dealing with my fellowman is selfishness.

Selfishness colors everything it touches. It detracts, afflicts, and destroys.

One reason, I am sure, that I find selfishness such an irritation is that I was reared in a home by parents who had the gladness of generosity.

They knew how to give. During the Depression, a man with a wife and four children was out of work. Dad and mother took in this family of six until they could get on their feet. It seemed the natural thing to do.

A cousin didn't have the money for a week of summer camp. Dad paid his way—with no mention of this unselfish act. Dad knew how to give.

And Christmas was the big event of the year! Dad had Wednesday afternoon off from the store, and for several weeks in advance he and mother would shop for their two sons, their daughters-in-law, and their grandchildren.

They shopped with their hearts—not with their pocketbooks—so they usually went beyond their means. So much did they give that my youngest child once asked me: "Are Granddaddy and Grandmother rich?"

"No," I answered, "far from it, but they have something even more valuable: they know how to give."

And always at Christmas, I reflect once again on their generosity. They knew the joy of giving.

And in this troubled day, the world would be a better place if many could discover the joy of giving. Selfishness, after all, is at the root of so many of the world's ills.

Perhaps that is what God was trying to tell us when He, as the greatest Giver of all, "so loved the world that he gave his only begotten Son."

This was the greatest gift the world has ever known. God knew how to give.

The Power of Spurgeon: the "Prince of Preachers"

Charles Haddon Spurgeon, nineteen-year-old country boy, had been a Christian for about three years when he arrived to occupy the pulpit of a tradition-bound church located in a large metropolitan area of London. The task must have been staggering for this inexperienced preacher, not yet dry behind his ministerial ears, who faced the challenge of bringing new life to a dying church.

On his first night in the boarding house, the old-timers kidded him, declaring that sophisticated worldly London would make short work of this country bumpkin. What happened in the next thirty years is a miraculous indication of heaven's own blessings upon the pastoral ministry of this man of God. A large tabernacle was constructed to hold thousands who came each week to hear Spurgeon preach. More than 10,000 persons came to Christ and united with the church.

Many opinions have been offered to explain the phenomenal success of this man who has been called the "Prince of Preachers." It has been suggested that his success was due to his striking use of illustrations which "locked in" the attention of his hearers. Some said it was the clarity and fresh style that brought his sermons right down to the needs of his congregation.

London newspapers, who sent journalists to report on his sermons, attributed his success to his earnestness, zeal, courage, sincerity, and genius for commanding an audience. But when asked about his success, Spurgeon humbly replied, "My people pray for me."

A group of preachers once came to his study before the beginning of a Sunday service and asked, "Where does your power come from?"

Spurgeon said, "Come with me," and he led the men down the stairs to the basement of the church. They began to murmur, "Oh, he is going to show us the electrical power room—we wanted to know the source of *his* power." In a moment, Spurgeon led them into a large room where many of his parishioners were on their knees fervently praying for God's blessings upon the service. "There," said Spurgeon, "is where the power comes from."

Doing What You Can

One major hindrance to the forward progress of so many churches is the fact that the average member of the congregation is not willing to do what he or she can do.

Pastors often hear a church member say, "You know, I just can't sing in the choir." All right, then what about teaching a Sunday School class, helping out in the nursery, or serving on a church committee?

Because you cannot do one thing does not excuse you from doing anything.

When Ramsey Pollard was pastor of the Bellevue Baptist Church in Memphis, a woman joined by letter from a country church in South Mississippi. Wearing a threadbare brown coat, print dress, tan cotton socks, and badly worn flat-heeled shoes, her face bore the deep weather lines acquired from years of working in the cotton field.

Obviously, she was fleeing the poverty of the rural South for what she hoped would be a better life in the city.

She came by the next day to see the pastor, and when she entered his study, Pollard, assuming that she was in need of help, was ready with a handout.

As she sat down, she said, "Pastor, yesterday morning in church you announced the Brotherhood was having its dinner Thursday night."

"Yes," said the pastor, "but it is for men."

"I understand," she said, "but I was thinking, now this is my church. I can't teach, I can't sing; I don't have money to give. All I can give is myself! Would you let me wash the dishes for that meeting, and that way I could feel I was doing something for my church and my Lord?"

She came Thursday night, washed the dishes, and continued week by week working in the church kitchen, washing dishes for her Lord and for her church!

This is the stewardship of life. We can all do something. And what we can do, we ought to do for the glory of God and the work of his Kingdom.

Solutions for Dealing with Difficult People

William Diehm has written a book, released by Broadman Press, on the subject *How to Get Along with Difficult People.*

The author, a retired clinical psychologist, says that everyone is a difficult person at one time or another. And sadly, in the case of a great many persons, it is more times than not.

Any veteran pastor who has dealt with a large number of persons over a long period of years would have to admit that, plainly and simply, some people were born with their nose out of joint.

They follow one central pattern in their lives: no matter what you suggest or bring up before them, they object to it.

In twenty-eight years in the pastorate, I discovered that the only thing you can do with difficult people such as these is to love them. You cannot please them and you cannot change them, but God can.

And no matter how hard you try, in your own strength, you cannot always love them. But you can love them in Christ.

Here is one other bit of advice: keep your sense of humor and your wits about you. I recall one incident in which a disturbed chairman of the social and entertainment committee came to the pastor. She was so upset that her eyes were blazing as she said, "I want you to know I will not be bullied!"

The pastor came right back with equal clarity as he replied, "And I will not be cowed."

They both laughed, shook hands, and a lasting friendship began.

This is not an easy world to live in. Situations are difficult. Some people are difficult.

But with your wits about you, plus a sense of humor and the strength of Jesus Christ, you can deal with some of the more difficult people, and situations can be laughed and loved away.

The Pause That Sharpens

This is such a harried, hectic, and hurried world that many of us have almost forgotten how to stop for a spell of rest and relaxation.

We sometimes forget that Jesus said to His disciples, "Come ye yourselves apart . . . and rest a while." (Mark 6:31)

Or as someone has put it, "Come apart to rest or face the risk of coming apart."

When we feel we are too busy to take a break, it might be well to also remember a pertinent story, originally told by Abraham Lincoln.

As it happened, two woodcutters had an all-day job to do.

One of the workers continued chopping all day, not even stopping for a moment's rest.

After eight hours of nonstop chopping, he had a large pile of logs.

In contrast, the other chopper would work for fifty minutes and then take a ten-minute break.

He worked calmly, deliberately, and steadily—but he seemed to do less work than his coworker.

However, the end of the day's work brought this surprise: the one who took the breaks had a much larger pile of logs than the woodcutter who had worked all day without stopping.

"How can this be possible?" asked the nonstop woodman as he collapsed in fatigue and disbelief.

"It's simple," replied the more relaxed woodcutter, "when I stopped to rest, I also sharpened my axe."

The pause that sharpens is important in the total Christian life.

We must work and work diligently. But we should also pause to sharpen the blade of prayer.

In every endeavor, we must work as if it all depended upon us, but frequently pause to pray in the knowledge that in reality, it all depends upon God.

And when life's day is over, the chore is done, and the wood is stacked, we can rest in the joy of knowing that "we have been found faithful as the sun goeth down."

The Sun Is Going to Rise

Sometime ago I came across some excellent advice which listed mistakes or pitfalls to avoid.

The suggestions are valuable to both clergymen and laypersons who have a sincere desire to march through life with victory and joy.

(1) Avoid the feeling of remorse over yesterday's failure. Yesterday is gone. Turn your failure over to the Lord, and your burden will be light.

(2) Avoid anxiety over today's problems. "This is the day which the Lord has made. Rejoice and be glad in it."

(3) Avoid worry over tomorrow's uncertainty. The future belongs to God. Commit your tomorrows to your Heavenly Father.

(4) Don't waste the moment's opportunity. Seize the opportunity of the moment and move on to achievement.

(5) Do not harbor resentment of another's success. The genuine person who is big of heart and spirit rejoices when others succeed.

(6) Do not be critical of a neighbor's imperfection. When one makes full recognition of all of his faults, he finds there is little time left to find fault with others.

(7) Do not be impatient with youth's immaturity. As the apostle Paul wrote, "When I was a child, I spoke as a child, I understood as a child, I thought as a child: but when I became a man, I put away childish things." Notice that the great apostle said, "When he became a man, he put away childish things." In God's great system, children are not to be little adults, and adults are not to be big children.

(8) Skepticism of the future. The most encouraging thought in the midst of life's perplexities is found in the words of the great old hymn "This Is Our Father's World."

(9) Avoid the pitfall of unbelief in God's providence. The grandson could hardly wait for morning's first light so that he could go fishing with his granddad.

"Granddaddy," asked the lad, "won't the sun ever come up?"

With the wisdom of age and faith, the old man replied; "It always has."

Monuments of Nothing

William Arthur Ward said he once heard this interesting definition of excuses: "Excuses are the tools with which persons with no purpose in view build for themselves great monuments of nothing."

Almost everyone lapses into the habit of making excuses. When a child, the excuse is "I'm too young."

And when time takes care of that, the excuse becomes "I'm too old."

Perhaps we need to reflect on the wise advice of Rudyard Kipling who said, "We have many reasons for failure, but not a single excuse."

Most successful persons are not good at excuse making because they get so little practice at it. However, failures are expert excuse-makers because it is a way of life with them.

The successful person is too busy to make excuses. He says, as a winner, "It may be difficult, but with God's help it's possible."

On the other hand, the failure says, "It's not possible—no matter who helps us—because it is too difficult."

In learning to apply the art of thinking with faith, we need to recognize the power of God in every situation—daily counting our blessings.

Few people on earth enjoy more comforts than do most Americans—and yet, even those who are greatly blessed are prone to find fault with life.

Jesus came "that we might have life and have it more abundantly." And this is the abundance that must be recognized.

If stress and strife cause us to become weak in the knees, perhaps we should drop on our knees and engage in serious prayer.

Swapping excuses for prayer would be a good exchange. And this should make possible a strong resolve to refuse to build monuments of nothing.

Instead, let's move forward in the strength of the Almighty, and use the tools at hand to build lasting monuments of service to God and man.

A Few More Days Remaining to "Straighten Up" for Christmas

In this festive season of the year, much attention is given to the number of shopping days remaining before Christmas. But what about other significant preparation that ought to be made for the coming of Christmas? There comes to mind the classic short story "The Luck of Roaring Camp," written by Bret Harte.

A moving story, it is an account of the birth of a baby boy on the American frontier. The mother, a disreputable person at best, was the "woman" of the mining camp who died in childbirth, leaving a healthy baby boy to be raised by the now all-male camp.

A meeting was called, and these crude, rough, hard men arrived at surprising decisions which marked the beginning of dramatic changes in the life of the camp. They considered employing a nurse to care for the baby, but eventually decided that a nice nurse wouldn't come to their camp, and they didn't want any women who weren't "nice" hanging around their baby. And so the camp transformation began.

The cabin set aside for Baby Tommy Luck, as they called him, was kept spotlessly clean and whitewashed. The newly purchased cradle made the other furniture appear woeful, so they replaced or fixed up the rest of the furniture in the cabin.

A rule was passed that anyone who wanted to hold the baby had to bathe and clean up for the privilege. This resulted in the overall cleanliness of the camp.

And since the baby needed sleep, the camp became quieter and rowdiness was soon a thing of the past. The story of the baby that was born into Roaring Camp is a story of the transformation and regeneration of people.

In a larger sense, it is a Christmas story that reminds us of the Christ child who came into an environment of sin and dirtiness and darkness. But as the only begotten Son of God, He changed sin into salvation, dirtiness into cleanliness, and darkness into light.

We all need days in which to "straighten up" for Christmas and the commemoration of the coming of the babe of Bethlehem.

As we herald once again the coming of the Christ Child, may we also welcome the departure from our lives of all these things which are not in keeping with his holy presence.

No Hiding Place

A pastor recently told of a couple in his church with the good health and well-deserved joy of celebrating their fifty-seventh wedding anniversary. At a small gathering held in honor of the occasion, the husband shared an account of his experience in shopping for a new car.

The old-timer was surprised at all of the new equipment and changes that had been made in the new model. He was even shown a new "talking car" by the salesman.

"Listen to this," said the salesman as he left the key in the ignition and opened the door. A woman's voice out of the dashboard said, "Your key is in the ignition!"

Then the salesman turned on the lights and opened the door. It happened again. The same woman's voice warned, "Your headlights are on!"

Continuing with the demonstration of the new automobile, the salesman started the engine with the car door open.

One more time there echoed inside the car the same woman's voice, "Your door is ajar!"

It was almost too much for the old fellow as he stared at the car in disbelief.

"Well," asked the salesman, "are you ready to drive it home?"

"No, sir," replied the elderly customer.

Pointing an accusing finger at the car, and with a twinkle in his eye, he said, "You see, I might go somewhere in this car—somewhere that's nobody's business but my own, come home, and that thing would tell my wife where I've been and what I've been up to. I'd rather have a car with a tight lip!"

The Bible also has some voices of warning—words of caution when our lives are not all they should be. One such warning is "Be sure your sin will find you out." (Numbers 32:23) And the Scripture voice also reminds us: "O, God, Thou knowest my foolishness; and my sins are not hidden from thee!" (Psalm 69:5) There is no hiding place from the follies of sin.

Vexation without Communication

Multiple present-day problems of home and family serve as reminders of the need in most families for expressed and communicated love.

Sincere affection is the cement that binds two people together as husband and wife. It is also the glue that holds the family together in the midst of stresses and strains of modern-day life.

There is a story making the rounds of a couple who went to Florida to celebrate their fiftieth wedding anniversary.

They viewed the beauty of the sea and sand, toured other scenic attractions, and had a great time on their second honeymoon.

Several times the devoted husband told his wife how much he loved her, how wonderful she was, and how fortunate he was to have been her husband for half a century.

On the last day of their visit, they had lunch in a restaurant overlooking the bay. As the husband looked across the table into the eyes of his wife, romantic feelings came again to his heart, and he wanted once more to express his appreciation for his wife.

So, with great sincerity, he said, "I'm proud of you!" She had grown a little hard of hearing and evidently missed the word that he had used as she replied, "I'm tired of you, too!"

Let us be certain our words of affection are clearly expressed and distinctly heard.

Praise What You Want to Raise

The importance of praise is often more readily recognized by those who receive it than by those who give it.

But this ought not to be. Since we cherish the times when we were praised for something we said or did, why don't we praise others more often than we do?

I have fond memories of one good woman in a congregation I once served as pastor. She carried on the ministry of encouragement.

And what a blessing she was! On most any given holiday, or special event, she would seize the opportunity to send a pretty card with a thoughtful word of appreciation.

In her wisdom, she knew that criticism tends to generate resentment and hostility which lessens self-confidence and effectiveness.

On the other hand, encouragement and appreciation motivate us and create enthusiasm for self-improvement.

I recall a wonderful layman in my very first student pastorate who used well the practice of praise. In fact, his words of encouragement and appreciation concerning my efforts at preaching were so timely and well done that he made of me a better preacher than I really was.

To know how and when to praise is a rare gift. Note these good habits of praise.

Praise efforts, not just accomplishments. Having someone appreciate what we have *tried* to do gives incentive to work even harder.

Praise initiative. Praise the person who goes the second mile without being asked.

Praise right now, before it is too late and the opportunity has passed forever.

Praising others for all that is in any way praiseworthy puts new joy into life and greater determination to do better.

Praise what you want to raise. Praise what you want to raise to new levels of achievement and success.

You, by this ministry of encouragement, will be looking up and causing others to look up.

Love Is More than a Word on a Greeting Card

I like Valentine's Day. I have appreciated it ever since my grammar school days when our teacher let us hand out valentines to all of our fellow class members.

As I became older and grew to be a bit more perceptive in my assessment of the event, I realized that its weakness was that for some it became a popularity contest to see who received the largest number of valentines.

And later in life, I came to know an even greater truth: "Love is more than a word on a greeting card."

The apostle Paul said it best in the wonderful "love chapter," 1 Corinthians 13:

Love suffereth long, and is kind; love envieth not;
love vaunteth not itself, is not puffed up. . . .
[Love] beareth all things, believeth all things,
hopeth all things, endureth all things.
Love never faileth; . . .
And now abideth faith, hope, love, these three;
but the greatest of these is love!

The measure of true Christian love is in its consistency and its endurance. Love never fails!

Notice: This does not indicate that in love everything always goes smoothly. Often the impediment to a good marriage is the wrong assumption that it should be free of all difficulties and should run like a smoothly working machine.

Truth is, the good marriage is not necessarily the one in which problems do not occur. The good marriage is one that succeeds in spite of difficulties because, as the Scripture says, "love endureth all things."

I like the sense of humor and the honesty of the husband who said: "When we were first married, we got along fine. But as we were leaving the church, a fuss began!"

The happy ending to this story is that this couple always worked out their problems because for them "love never fails."

You see, love is more than a word on a valentine card.

A Little Less Starch, Please

One observer of the current religious scene has written about a certain type of Christian who gives the impression of "having been starched before having been washed."

"A little on the stiff side" would be a charitable assessment of such a person.

There is an attendant danger in such a condition, inasmuch as starch is usually quite resistant to the grace of God.

For example, too much starch can cause a person to have an image of self that is a long way from reality.

Self-satisfaction leads to further deception and a lack of awareness of one's deep spiritual needs.

Life can then become a kind of joyless, juiceless conformity to a starched self-image.

When the preacher enters the pulpit on Sunday morning, looks out over the congregation and sees all the heavily starched glum faces lined out before him, the temptation would be to ask, "Does it really hurt that much to be a Christian?"

Then, too, the overly starched person may also have a tendency to be judgmental of others.

Sitting up tall, straight, and starched makes it easier to find fault with one's fellowman.

Of course, like the mote and beam in the eye, as recorded in the Scripture, it could be said that detecting the starch of fault in another person may be an indication of the oversupply of starch in your own soul.

No matter what the TV commercials may claim, "ring around the collar" is not as serious as too much starch in the spiritual collar, resulting in a stiff-necked, unhappy Christian prevented from enjoying the fulfilled life in Christ.

The solution is a simple one. When passing through God's heavenly laundry, be sure to make this request: "A little less starch, please!"

Healthy Concern for Others

We now have it on good authority that an unselfish attitude of concern for others is the healthy way of life.

To be indifferent to the needs of others is to know the truth of the saying: one who is wrapped up in himself makes a very small package.

Dr. Karl Menninger was once asked what a person should do if he felt a nervous breakdown coming on.

The famous psychiatrist replied, "Do this: get out of your house, go across the railroad tracks to a deprived, poverty-stricken area, find someone in need, and do something for him."

It is a stinging condemnation to realize that many of us are not always quick to recognize the needs of those around us.

In reading some biographical material of the late New York City Mayor Fiorello La Guardia, it was interesting to note that when he was in office during the years of 1933 to 1945, he became known as an efficient reformer who kept in touch with the people and their problems.

As mayor, La Guardia liked to keep in touch with all the various departments under his supervision.

One time he chose to preside over night court. It was a bitterly cold winter night, and a frightened, trembling man was brought before him charged with stealing a loaf of bread. His family, he said, was starving.

With a tone of compassion and concern in his voice, La Guardia declared, "I have to punish you—there can be no exception to the law. I fine you $10."

However, even as he said this, La Guardia was reaching into his own pocket for the money. "Here's $10 to pay your fine—which I now remit," he said.

"Furthermore," he declared, "I am going to fine everybody in this courtroom $1 for living in a city where a man has to steal bread in order to eat. Mr. Bailiff, collect the fines and give them to the defendant!"

The hat was passed, and the money given to the needy man who went out into the winter night with a new warmth in his heart.

But there was also a warmer, healthier feeling in the hearts of those who had acted to meet the needs of their fellow man.

Great Commitment Means Great Churches!

Many organizations, including the church, are hindered and held back from great success because of the lack of commitment on the part of the participants.

All the way from the Sunday School to the choir, there are those church staff members who can tell you of teachers who do not show up to teach and singers who fail to show up to sing.

Many staff members can identify with this story:

The conductor of the local orchestra was terribly frustrated because at each rehearsal at least one musician was absent.

The concert was only two days away, and the conductor feared the orchestra would not be ready for the performance.

But he decided to handle it in a positive way, so at the final rehearsal with everyone present, the conductor publicly thanked the pianist, who had not missed a single practice session.

"Well, it's the least I could do," replied the pianist, "considering I won't be able to play at the concert tonight."

Staying with the task and seeing it through to completion can make the difference between failure and success in the work of the church.

A church is truly great when its membership walks in commitment with God and in fellowship with one another.

A great church is a committed church where Sunday attendance is not affected by the weather and where enthusiasm on Sunday evening runs as high as that on Sunday morning.

A great church is a church where a committed membership serves to the glory of God, and where every victory is a cause for rejoicing in every service.

And a great church is a church where the commitment of the membership continues to express itself in good and bad times through sacrificial giving and service.

Present in Spirit, Absent in Body

In more than twenty-eight years as pastor of four different congregations, I am quick to admit that I never achieved any noteworthy results with members of my churches who said, "I'm sorry I can't be present with you in the service, but I will be with you in spirit."

I must confess that, although my eyes anxiously searched every pew, I was never able to locate their "spirits."

The only one I ever heard of who won out in the "I'll be with you in spirit" game was a young lady who was going around town selling tickets for a special concert to benefit the high school band.

She accepted the challenge of calling on the "tightest man" in town with the hope of selling him two tickets. The old fellow, with years of practice at protecting his pocketbook, began to offer excuses: "Oh," he said, "I'm sorry, I already have an engagement that night—but I will be with you in spirit."

"That's fine," snapped the young lady, "tickets are $10 each. Where do you want your spirit to sit?"

Good effort notwithstanding, the truth is the blessings to be had from any event fall to those who are there in person.

Various attendance-promotion ideas are attempted such as this most unusual offer that appeared in one church newsletter: "Why not tackle regular attendance on a trial basis? If you don't like what you hear on any Sunday, your sins will be quickly refunded."

It is amazing that in perhaps the most insane, deranged time in all of history, many persons see no need to join others in a place dedicated to the worship of Almighty God.

Some think it silly to go to church and sing praises and offer prayers to God. They think it is tiresome—even a waste of time.

But all would have to admit that much difficulty comes to people in their lives and honesty requires that you ask, What gets them through it? Where is the victory?

The honest answer is that triumph over trials comes to many because of a great faith made stronger and nurtured in the regular experience of worship of the true and loving God.

And that is worship in both body and spirit.

The Difficulty of Conducting an "Adult Nursery"

A well-known pastor and veteran of many years of service in various churches—one who had spent his time "in the trenches" caught up in every conceivable church fuss and conflict—was once asked what he considered to be the most difficult assignment a minister has in all of his broad range of activities.

Pausing for only a moment's thought, he stared straight ahead with a twinkle in his eye and answered, "As a longtime pastor of the local church, the most difficult part of my work was being expected to conduct an 'adult nursery'."

This is a point well taken. All may begin, as Paul said, as "babes in Christ," but to remain in this state of immaturity is to be a problem to oneself and to everyone with whom one comes in contact.

"Oh, grow up," is not a word needed only from parent to child. It is a word for all who would seek that essential attribute for the good life: maturity.

Note these points of maturity. If you can see someone else take credit for a piece of work for which you have labored long and hard and feel no bitterness, you are living in a rare circle of Christian maturity.

As someone wisely said, "There's no telling how much good could be done in the world if we'd stop worrying about who gets the credit."

If you can see another chosen for a job that you yourself are better qualified to do, and then pray for the success of that person, that is maturity.

If you can hear another argue a point of view that is contrary to your own and respect his right to his opinion, that is maturity.

If you can accept someone's criticism of you—even though it is unkind, unfair, and even untrue—without resentment, then you are practicing Christian maturity.

And to do so—as you turn that heavy burden of resentment over to the Lord—will assure you of a lighter, smoother, happier, journey through life.

Gift for the Father

During a family Bible conference in Toccoa, a young boy came by the book table and began a careful examination of every volume displayed there.

His was an important mission. He was there for a serious purpose. He wanted to buy a book to take home to his daddy.

Asking prices of the books, he then checked his pocketbook. Would the remaining amount be enough for his purchase?

Knowing the temptation of the snack bar, he said, "I want to be sure and buy a book tomorrow before all my money is gone."

Next day, he returned to the book table. His love for his Dad had won over any other places his money might have gone.

He conferred with the one who was in charge of book sales, and decided to purchase one of my books. Wanting the book autographed, the youngster found me in the dining hall and said, "I was told if I got one of your books, you would autograph it."

"Oh, yes," I said, "I'd be happy to do that for you."

The book was signed, and the boy walked away with a smile and the satisfaction that goes with the act of doing something for someone else—the unselfish gesture of giving a part of yourself for someone you love.

There are so many things that clamor for our funds in this day, things that bring pleasure for the moment. But always, there is that better place, that better use of our money.

With this young fellow, the transfer of funds was made even more special by the fact that it was a gift for his father.

In a larger sense that should be the motive and mission of all God's children: to bring a gift, something of themselves, to the heavenly Father, the most loving and generous Father of all.

As we do this, we, too, shall have that glowing unselfish feeling, the feeling that goes with bringing a gift to the Father.

Tearing Down a Pastor or Building Up a Pastor?

According to new research, the most common way to resolve serious conflict in churches is to force out the pastor.

Because of a misinterpretation of what may be the true difficulty within the church, forced termination of ministers is a problem that won't go away.

One practice of many congregations is to make certain the pastor gets the blame for everything that goes wrong.

I heard one church member confirm this by saying, "The preacher just let the church go down."

So far as I can determine, this is the only thing for which many congregations are willing to give the pastor full credit.

I have always felt that there are striking similarities between coaching a football team and pastoring a local church.

In both lines of work, you can be given a new car one year and the very next year ridden out of town on a rail.

Some congregations need to be reminded that not only are there ways to tear down a pastor, there are ways to build up a pastor.

True, a great pastor with the blessings of God builds the church, but it is no less true that a great church builds the pastor.

Congregations, please heed these suggestions.

(1) Build the pastor's power by praying for him. If you must whisper about anything, whisper a prayer.

(2) Build the pastor's reputation by speaking well of him. Brag on him, and he may become the pastor and preacher you want him to be.

(3) Build his leadership by cooperating with him. No one can lead unless there are those who will follow.

(4) Build his pulpit power by hearing him. Full pews are an encouragement to him. No one likes to speak to a "lumberyard," no matter how highly polished it may be.

(5) But all in all, the most important service you can perform for your pastor-preacher is to follow the Christ he preaches—and the constructive result in building up all things will be wondrous to behold.

Service More than Style

The story has it that once a man attended a fair and saw a stable boy leading a beautiful, well-groomed horse.

Catching up to the boy and the horse, he asked, "Is that a saddle horse?"

"No, sir," was the reply. "This horse will buck off a saddle. No one can stay on his back."

"Tell me, then," inquired the man, "is he suited to pulling a carriage?"

"No," answered the boy. "He was hitched up once and it upset him so much that he kicked up a fuss and made kindling wood of the vehicle he should have pulled."

"Well, then, what is he good for? Why is he here?" the man asked.

The boy's answer was simple and direct, "Why, man, he is good for style. Just look: he is here for the fine picture he makes!"

That same man was attending a worship service in a magnificent church building and watched as people dressed in fine clothes came into the morning service.

Seeing the young pastor near the front, he asked, "Are all of these people workers in the church? Do they pull their share of the load?"

"No," answered the pastor, sadly. "I am sorry to say that they do not."

"Well," asked the man, "do most of them visit the sick, witness to the lost, and give freely of their possessions?"

"No," replied the preacher, "at most, only a few practice good church membership and dedicated stewardship."

As he turned away, the man felt compelled to say to himself, "Just like the beautiful horse at the fair—nothing but style."

Carrying out the Great Commission requires more than style.

Witnessing to the lost demands more than keeping up appearances.

Honest stewardship of possessions is more than head held high; it has to do with open hearts and open hands.

Where the work of Christ through the church is concerned, service is more than style.

Procrastination Is the Enemy of Progress

It was recently reported on a news broadcast that the National Association of Procrastinators finally got around to having their convention.

I understand it comes later every year. As with all other endeavors, they put it off as long as they can.

Whatever else you may say about procrastination, it should be recognized as an enemy of progress. It has held up and held back many worthy projects.

It is the prime enemy of achievement. It is the failing of many and a blessing to none.

The Bible gives no comfort to the procrastinator, for it clearly urges action and declares: "Now is the time. Today is the day."

Those who have the bad habit of delaying everything need to understand that the great dividing line between success and failure can be expressed in seven damaging words: "I could not get around to it."

Unfortunate are the words "He was going to do something great—but he had to put it off until tomorrow."

In fact, he told everybody that he was going to be all that a mortal could be—tomorrow.

And none would be braver or stronger than he—if they could just wait until tomorrow.

He would make his plans and stack up all the letters he needed to write—but not until tomorrow.

He would be more thoughtful and loving toward his fellowman—if he could just work it into his schedule tomorrow.

And more importantly, he was going to do more for God and the church—tomorrow.

Sad to say, that although he had the best of intentions, they went the way of procrastination, and, as always, tomorrow never came.

The Art of Striving

When it comes to leadership and success, experts insist that millions of persons in every walk of life have never tried to reach high goals that were reachable or solve problems that were solvable because they were told—and believed—"It couldn't be done." This is often true in church work. As the little verse so aptly expresses it:

When fires of enthusiasm burn with heat intense,
Someone takes the hose of common sense,
And puts out the fire with little expense.

Sad to say, there are those who consider it their life's work to throw cold water on every new project and dampen enthusiasm at every exciting turn in the road.

In a reversal of the usual progressive procedure, they follow the practice of "accentuating the negative and eliminating the positive" from every worthy endeavor.

At the other extreme, according to the late Vance Havner, are those dear souls who have all the dealings and doings of God catalogued, correlated, and computerized, and can give you all the answers wrapped up in a box with a ribbon on it.

Trouble is, these folks just haven't been far enough on their pilgrim's journey down life's highway. God does not operate on our timetable, and some of His operations don't add up on our computers.

The little boy who didn't understand why God put so many vitamins in spinach and so few in ice cream had a pretty good idea that life doesn't always work out according to our plans.

The happy medium in all of this is to face life and its challenges with enthusiasm and courage born of a great faith in Almighty God.

My faith is this: People who stay together with God and each other can do anything. Hear the poet:

I've learned a bit of wisdom
Along life's often rocky way;
This simple guide for living,
Be grateful to God for today.

I've learned a vital lesson
Worth more than gems or gold;
I've learned from tribulations
To bend, but not to fold.

Roses in December

Someone has said, "God gave us memory so that we might have roses in December."

These words have a beautiful meaning. They mean that we fill our minds during the passing years with choice thoughts and our heads and hands with helpful ministries, and our hearts with strong faith and commitment. Then when the winter of life comes—times of solitude, disappointment, tragedy, sorrow—there would be light at eventide, and roses fragrant and beautiful.

The elderly widow of a minister was told that she was going blind. When she reported the news to her neighbor, there was no bitterness in her voice.

Instead she spoke with gratitude of how God had allowed her to discover her misfortune several months before the total eclipse of sight.

"You see," she said humbly, "I am gathering bits of loveliness to lay by store against the day of my blindness. I am walking more often among my flowers, etching their beauty upon my heart. I am looking with more appreciation on the gorgeous sunsets and am reading God's Word more intently, hoping to chisel its truths in my heart."

Roses in December! She would have them when the darkness of life's long winter night closed in upon her.

This was what our Saviour had in view when he urged the "laying up for ourselves treasures in heaven where neither moth nor rust do corrupt and where thieves do not break in and steal."

But understand this: if the queen of summer flowers is to adorn our December, it must be nourished, tended, pruned, and guarded.

We must work at it. One cannot store up that of which he has never taken hold.

If we are to lay up a good foundation against the time to come—the winters of life—then we must cultivate that which is imperishable while it is still summer.

For if we fill our minds and hearts with the foundation of a strong, abiding faith, we can know that even the coldest winter winds of difficulty cannot prevent us from having our roses in December.

Sense of Humor Needed by Everyone

Frequently, earthquakes are reported in our nation and around the world, and these are always episodes of great concern for all of us.

But it seems, on the other hand, that we also ought to be concerned that we do everything we can to see that this tired old world has a genuine mirthquake that would bring more laughter and joy into our lives.

Of all people to be pitied in this troubled and heartbreaking day, there are those who do not have a sense of humor.

However, somewhere in my reading, I came across the good news that although some persons may not have been born with the ability to laugh, it is possible for them to develop a sense of humor.

If you find it difficult to see the funny side of life and you cannot easily break into laughter, here is what the experts recommend:

Be familiar with your laughter profile. Know what makes you laugh.

Look and listen hard for the point of the joke. Don't just stand there with a confused expression on your face, uttering the words, "I don't get it."

Try to warm up to the humorous. Start thinking about something funny. If it doesn't seem funny at first, stay with it.

And do this for yourself: during the tensest part of your day, take a five minute humor-meditation break. Think of a humorous situation or a funny play on words.

For example, in facing retirement from the usual long workday, this comes to mind: It is said that hard work never killed anybody. But then again, resting is responsible for very few casualties.

When all is said and done, look for something to smile and laugh about.

Surely, when the Bible urged us "to make a joyful noise unto the Lord," it included more than singing. It meant laughter, too.

Persevering through Failure

It is not always what happens to us—but how we react to what happens to us that is of the utmost importance in our lives. For some persons, the troubles of life seem to build strength of character. The fire tempers the steel. Here is a case in point.

When he was seven years old, his family was forced out of their home, and he had to go to work to help bring in needed financial support.

At age nine, his mother died.

At age twenty-two, he lost his job as a store clerk. He had hoped to go to law school, but his education wasn't good enough.

At twenty-three, he went into debt to become a partner in a small store. However, at twenty-six, his business partner died, leaving him with a huge debt which took years to repay.

He also was "unlucky in love," as the saying goes. At age twenty-eight, after courting a girl for four years, he asked her to marry him. His failures continued: she said, "No."

Then, at thirty-seven, it seemed that his fortune was turning more in his favor. In his third attempt, he was elected to Congress. But two years later the dark cloud of disappointment came over him once again: he failed to be reelected.

At forty-five, he ran for the Senate and lost; and at forty-seven, he failed as the vice presidential candidate. At forty-nine, he again ran for the Senate and lost.

But after all of these reversals, he was elected president of the United States at age fifty-one.

His name was Abraham Lincoln, who persevered through his failures until at last he succeeded.

With all of his failures and disappointments, it would have been easy to yield to the temptation to take the easy way, forget principle, and "do anything to win." But he would not go that way.

So strong was his character that as president he declared, "You will never get me to support a measure or anything which I believe to be wrong, although by doing so, I might accomplish that which I believe to be right."

Failures and hardships can strengthen character—if we allow them to do so.

Futility of Worry

This frantic and frenzied age in which we live could be remembered for the three distinctives of "Worry, hurry, and bury."

But no matter how futile, it seems that almost everyone engages in the first: worry. There have been various responses to the problem of worry. One man said, "Worry is bad for the digestion; I do as little of it as possible."

Another unusual old fellow said, with tongue in cheek, "I decided a long time ago that worry wasn't good for you, so I decided to just put the burden of all my worries on my cat." Continuing, he said, "Of course, it's been good for me, but awfully hard on my cat."

Be that as it may, there are countless persons who wake up in the middle of the night in a cold sweat, worrying about a problem they face the next day or one that may present itself in the near or distant future. No problem was ever solved by worrying, and yet worry continues to be a heavy energy consumer for many persons. Think on this: if all of the effort expended on worry was channeled into constructive approaches at finding solutions, we would be healthier and happier.

Here are suggestions for minimizing worry.

Don't continue to go over and over the same problem. Come quickly to a decision. Most worry is caused by not being able to decide.

When you've made your decision, stick to it. Always remember that clear thinking is constructive. Worry is destructive.

And most important, follow the good advice of the wonderful old hymn: "Take your burdens to the Lord and leave them there."

And after all, this is the wisest thing to do when you consider the spiritual exercise of affirming these truths:

The Lord operated the world quite well without me long before I came on the scene. And He will continue to operate the world long after I am gone.

This being true, it stands to reason that I ought to stop struggling with the world's problems and let the Lord be in charge now.

Growing Old

According to a friend, you can tell you are growing old when you get up in the morning and almost everything hurts, and what doesn't hurt doesn't work.

In fact, your back goes out more than you do. Also, you know you are getting old when the only gleam in your eye is caused by the sun reflecting off your bifocals.

Old age has found you when all your address book contains is names ending with M.D.

The years are piling up for parents when their children begin to look middle-aged.

Retirees tell me that it is also a clear indication of the results of old age when upon giving up their work, they decide to enjoy the luxury of procrastination—but never get around to it.

As for an old-timer, you also spend a lot of time in your rocking chair and sometime you even feel inspired to make the effort to rock.

And as disappointing as it is to admit, with the accumulation of years of wisdom, you now feel that you know all the answers—but nobody is willing to ask you a question.

Still and all, we can look back on the past with satisfaction and look forward with anticipation if we, in our Christian conversion experience, "put off the old man and put on the new man in Christ."

We can then walk with heavenly assurance toward that ever brighter day.

"He Rose Again, You Know"

A man was walking down a street in Chicago when in a store window he saw a vivid painting portraying the crucifixion. Gazing intently at the pictorial display, he became aware that at his side was another spectator: a dirty, poorly clad boy of the street. Touching the boy on the shoulder, the man asked, "Son, what does it mean?"

"That man is Jesus," the boy replied, "and them others is Roman soldiers, and the woman what's crying is his mother." And he added with a sob, "They killed him."

Finally, the man turned and walked down the street, but in a few minutes he heard footsteps running after him, and the boy shouting, "Mister, mister, I forgot to tell you, but He rose again!"

No matter how many messages are prepared and sermons preached, this remains and ever shall be the message of Easter: "He rose again!"

And, as Phillips Brooks said, "The great Easter truth is not that we are to live newly after death—that is not the great thing—but that we are to be new here and now by the power of the resurrection; not just that we are to live forever as that we are to live nobly now because through Christ we are to live forever."

This incident speaks to this truth. It was bedtime for the little boy, and his father knelt down to join him in his prayers: "Now, I lay me down to sleep; I pray the Lord my soul to keep. If I should *wake before I die. . . .*"

Then, embarrassed, he apologized, "Oh, Daddy, I messed up and said it wrong."

"Not at all, Son," said his father, "my deepest longing for both of us is that we may wake up before we die."

After all, that is the Good News of Easter. This is the time to come alive. The joy of Easter is that righteousness triumphs. Evil may have its terrible day, but goodness wins. Evil forces may win some battles, but godly forces shall win the war!

In the power of the risen Christ, we must march onward and upward. Let this be our theme: If I should wake before I die, then I must now live and serve the victorious Christ.

He rose again, you know!

Topical Index